T0077918

THE POWER OF CREATIVE THINKING

THE SECRET TO ATTRACTING AND MANIFESTING YOUR IDEAL LIFE

RISHI AKMAN

BALBOA.PRESS

A DIVISION OF HAY HOUSE

Balboa Press books may be ordered through booksellers or by contacting:

Balboa Press
A Division of Hay House
1663 Liberty Drive
Bloomington, IN 47403
www.balboapress.com
844-682-1282

Print information available on the last page.

ISBN: 978-1-9822-6692-9 (sc)
ISBN: 978-1-9822-6693-6 (e)

Balboa Press rev. date: 04/15/2021

PRAISE FOR THE POWER OF CREATIVE THINKING

•■•

The author presents an in-depth approach for achieving spiritual growth and psychological development. This book is amazing!
—Terrence M. Houston, psyche nurse, LPN

The Power of Creative Thinking will teach you how to turn defeat into victory, lack into prosperity, fear into faith, and resentment into love.
—Eric Scott, founder and CEO of In Time of Need Health Care Agency

The Power of Creative Thinking has a very profound message. I foresee it changing countless lives for those who embrace it.
—John L. Avery

The Power of Creative Thinking will transform every aspect of your life in a powerful and positive way if you practice its principles.

—Janie York

The principles in this book helped me to unravel the many layers of false perceptions that I had initially viewed the world through. It provided mental clarity when I slipped out of the present moment. This book is a priceless tool, which continuously guides me into the *here and now*.

—Amanda Poling

The author has an extraordinary ability to understand the psychological makeup of people and the skill to express the solutions in layman's so that the average person can understand. It comes through crystal clear in this book. Do not miss it!

—Marvin L. Baker, ADC-T

CONTENTS

•■•

FOREWORD

I am honored to welcome you, the seeker of truth, to the Christ consciousness's great teachings, regarding the power of creative thinking. When they are properly understood and executed in accordance with universal laws, you will be able to rise above the limitations, struggles, and hardships of life. They will free you from fret, fear, and grief and give you faith, love, and happiness.

Most people are searching for truth. They hope to acquire its meaning as life unfolds. There are many ways to approach the quest for truth. Some of these are more constructive and illuminating than others are. However, the outcome of the search varies from person to person, primarily due to the nature of each person's calling.

Truth alone bestows real peace and joy within our beings, which is our spiritual inheritance. Even if we do not have a clear understanding of the things that constitute truth or the event that first causes it, we as incarnated beings continually gravitate toward truth—continuously being an expression of truth's light. The quest for truth has one destination but many routes. These routes are all configured by spiritual and universal laws, just as the physical plane is governed by the laws of energy, thermodynamics, and motion.

So we journey the path of spiritual planes, which governs all other laws that allow us to experience the attributes of love, oneness, interdependence, justice, and harmony. However, if these laws are ignored or violated, we will suffer. The same applies to our physical bodies. So then, it is important to avoid any kind of unhealthy activity so that the body will not prematurely deteriorate. In fact, if we choose to practice things that adversely affect our physical vessels' function, as well as our spiritual progress, it can have devastating outcomes.

In order to avoid such results, you must adhere to the underlining principles that promote good health. Where do we find these key principles? These principles are hidden in illuminated texts, which have been handed down too many cultures over the past millennia and veiled in symbols, allegory, mythology, spiritual languages, and rituals.

Today, we see this great secret of arcane knowledge gradually being unveiled within major religions, including the Christian faith. This book serves as another source to unveil those secret principles. It helps the serious seeker ascend spiritually into higher realms of divine consciousness, where truth subsists.

Several years ago, my destiny's path conjoined with the author's path. Upon first meeting him, I knew that I was in the company of a kindred spirit. Over many years, my experience with Seth has always been marked by the clarity of his analytical mind, profundity of his thoughts, solidity of his integrity, and serenity of his compassion. Rishi Akman is the personification of applying the principles that are elucidated in this book. He is proof of higher conscious living.

This book will serve as a guiding light and help the reader better position himself or herself for an empirical dawning of wisdom and understanding. Optimistically, this will lead the seeker into a deeper awareness of the Spirit of God and the Christ consciousness within. Peace and joy are available to the sincere seeker, and they are found in the journey.

—Dr. James Brown, MD

ACKNOWLEDGMENTS

●■●

I am fortunate to be sharing something that is of great value and will help so many people who are living in bad situations. Doing so has made my life satisfying, in ways that I never would have imagined. This book is a result of people participating and sharing their ideas and experiences with a similar passion.

Anything of great significance is achieved only with the collaborative efforts of like-minded and inspired individuals. First, I would like to express my heartfelt gratitude to God, who divinely inspired me to share this message in book form.

Also, I give special thanks to Ashley, a remarkable woman whom I love dearly, for her incredible support and encouragement through this entire writing process.

I want to thank Charlie Baker and Bob Vancuren, who are partly responsible for financing the publishing of this book.

Next, thank you, Omar Sharif, who was a man of vast wisdom, served as a mentor, and was a powerful masculine presence within this universe. His teachings contributed to my spiritual evolution.

I want to thank my son, Chris, who often kept me in prayer mode. This played a major role in the developing of this book.

I also want to thank Adam Houston and Herman McWhorters for their ongoing encouragement.

Thank you, Shirley Stringer, who spent many hours typing and formatting this book in the beginning phases.

I extend a sincere thanks to those who took time out of their busy schedules to submit their testimonials. They shared the profound principles that deeply touched and/or transformed their lives.

I also give thanks to my close friends and associates, who were instrumental and supportive in my writing of this unique book. I want to thank all the members of my inner circle, who rendered enormous encouragement and support in this lengthy endeavor.

My sincere thanks go to Herb Bias, the extraordinary photographer who produced my front cover photo shot.

Thank you to Francisco Yap, the representative of Shaker Heights Filipino community and Juan Sunga, founder, and CEO of the W-4 Alliance, which is located in Manila, Philippines.

Finally, to you the chosen reader, I am persuaded that nothing happens by chance. All is in divine order and perfectly orchestrated by God for your higher good, as well as your spiritual growth and development, whether you are aware of it or not. For this very reason, you are reading this book. You were destined to read its life-changing message at this precise moment.

Together, we can serve as inspirations to help awaken others from their mental sleep to the reality of the Christ-divine consciousness so that they might personally attain an authentic transformation.

INTRODUCTION

———————————— •■• ————————————

Bookstores are full of self-help books. More are being packed on the shelves weekly. You may be asking yourself, *what makes this book so special? Why should I read this one?* I am glad you asked. This book is about results and not only about theories. Much of its content is based on my personal life experiences.

If you want a life that is filled with inner peace, joy, and contentment, this book is for you. If you want to heal from past emotional hurts, which may have been imposed on or even self-inflicted, this book is for you. If you want to leave behind the old mentality of limitations and lack, this book is for you. More importantly, if you want to explore the most profound depths of who you are while discovering your place in this vast universe, this book is for you!

I challenge you to step out in faith and reach for the stars. Even if you land on the moon, you are still in a good position to experience unlimited possibilities. This is the moment when you take full control of your destiny and have the life that you have always wanted. It is all yours, so go, experience it, and grab it!

This book is a direct result of meditation, contemplation, and realization. It rests on the biblical premise that God created existence by His thoughts, speech, and actions and that His kingdom resides within us (see Genesis 1:1–27 and Luke 17:21). This book was written mainly for those who are searching for a deeper understanding of who they really are. To that end, my intention is to keep the content direct and clear.

However, please understand that no attempt is being made to convince or persuade anybody of anything, influence anyone's thinking, or argue about different opinions or points of views. If what I have written encourages and inspires the reader to clarify his or her own understanding in regard to that person's existence and ability to create a better life, this book has served its purpose.

Its esoteric message is not a complete exposition on the much written about subject. But it is suggestive as well as explanatory. Its aim is to motivate both men and women to journey and discover the true essence of their beings. When people discover themselves, it is the greatest discovery in the world. There is ancient proverb that says, "Know thyself." Therein, the foundation of success, health, and an abundant life lies.

Very few people in today's society, even the highly educated, know about the spiritual forces that are behind their success or the power that they possess. This inherent power exists within all of us, in the form of hidden talents and abilities, which lie dormant and wait to surface. Only through the adequate appropriation of these gifts is one able to blossom into one's full potential of creativity. This innate power can literally transform your entire life.

On the other hand, the same power can adversely work against you if it is used destructively, resulting in destitution, despondency, or death. Even with good intentions, the lack of knowledge and improper application of power can result in undesired consequences. For example, there is a biblical account in Acts 19:11–16 that describes seven men called "the sons of Sceva," who attempted to imitate Paul's innate power and ability to cast out evil spirits. Instead, they were beaten by a maniac who was possessed by similar spirits.

Therefore, it is important to understand this God-given power and its uses so that we will not misuse it, but we will avoid unnecessary suffering. More importantly, this spiritual power is used for God's divine plan.

In His creative state, God gave Himself a desire to impart His attributes and characteristics to a receptive vessel, which was man. According to scripture, creation was created by God, through imagery and speech. God began organizing a shapeless and barren earth. He called the physical world into being out of nothingness.

He provided light and air. He separated land from water, which was followed by the creation of plants, animals, and humans—the pinnacle of that creation. Creation is an integrated manifestation of matter, energy, space, and time within the universe.

Man and woman are the crowning achievements of God's handiwork. God gave them dominion over the natural world so that they might reign and rule in an orderly fashion. Because we bear God's image, we are His visible representatives on earth, who express the essence of His likeness.

God passed down His fatherly traits to Adam, giving him authorization and authority to take dominion over the earth and replenish its inhabitants. Therefore, you are created in the same fashion, form, and image as was Adam was. You are infused with the attributes of God like a child is to his or her natural father.

Through this divine inheritance, you are authorized to create as the Creator did and as if He were present Himself. He imagined the universe and humankind, speaking both into existence. In the same manner, Jesus, the Christ, exemplified this inherent ability throughout His entire mission on earth, as did other masters. He changed water into wine, opened blind eyes, healed all manner of diseases, calmed the raging seas, and raised the dead. Jesus taught His disciples that they possessed the same innate abilities. He admonished them to follow His pattern.

Jesus was the perfect example because He personified the characteristics and nature of God while functioning as a human being. In fact, you have identical inherent capabilities to His. You have the power to create whatever you choose to experience: a better life, harmonious relationships, more finances, a better job, etc. This can be achieved by tapping into the essence of your being, wherein lies the creative power of the Creator.

Now is the time to accept your full birthright from God, which will allow you to perform great exploits in the earthly realm. So do not wait any longer to start the creative process. The following pages will show you how to identify who you really are and how to create your ideal life. Also, you will discover a blueprint for using your imagination, words, and actions to formulate and manifest your ideal life.

But before you turn this page, know that you are about to walk down a passageway of a once-veiled knowledge. You will learn higher principles of truth and life, as taught by the Master, Jesus Christ. I humbly ask that you approach it with an open mind because some ideas might be new to you, and at first, your conscious mind might reject it.

However, if you mentally set aside your biased opinions and judgments while reading this material, the Spirit will enable you to see the things that are written and certain truths with deeper clarity. Whether you are a Baptist, Pentecostal, Protestant, Catholic, Jew, Muslim, or person of another religious faith, these universal principles hold truth for all. Presumably, we all pray to the same God, even though we may use different terms, titles, and labels in an attempt to describe His existence.

If you are familiar with these concepts and ideas, it can only increase your understanding, growth, and development. As you continue to engage in the text, your spiritual journey will become clear, leading you into a destiny that flows with abundant blessings.

The spirit behind the content of this book in conjunction with your openness will liberate you from the mental and emotional bondages that you may be experiencing. After reading this book, my sincere hope is that you will have gained a better understanding of the person that you are, your inherent ability to create, and ways to develop Christ consciousness within yourself, for the purpose of achieving self-mastery and being of service to others. The choice of how you will create certain conditions that attract your desired lifestyle is yours. You now hold your destiny in your own hands. So turn the page and start your life-changing journey.

CHAPTER 1

TWO ASPECTS OF TRUTH

— •■• —

Absolute Truth and Relative Truth

The quest for absolute truth is a personal journey. Only the seeker can travel it. However, while in search of such truth, there is a great possibility that the seeker will experience inner uniqueness. The seeker realizes that he or she is the builder of the inner self, by virtue of the thoughts that are chosen to be entertained. The mind is the master architect, the inner molder of character, and the outer molder of circumstances. Those who have been cast into the fire of ignorance can now be molded into their mental blueprints.

So it becomes increasingly important to maintain the inward ascension toward this abstract truth. It will allow you to discover yourself in new ways, such as knowing who you are, why you are here, and the meaning of life. These questions will be addressed in more detail later.

You will understand the power of thought. You will learn how to think effectively so that you can enhance your present living conditions. In addition, you will learn how to operate as God's cocreator and to create your own experiences by aligning and attuning yourself to your feelings with your thoughts.

As you think and feel, you create. Thinking and feeling are always active in your life. You do both every moment of the day, which means you create moment by moment, although you are unaware of it, and you do not realize the outcomes of this creative phenomenon and the direct impact that it will have on your life.

Thoughts are like seeds. They are enclosed by amassed energy and ready to germinate and sprout forth from the soil in which they were planted. You do not have to understand the science of how this evolving process works, but you need to cultivate the seed of thought with good intentions if you want to create a desirable experience.

The aptitude to create (manifest) is available to every living soul. Three components must be fully understood before the creative process can be initiated: clarity, duration, and intention. For a thought to manifest as reality, it must first be a clear, precise image with a sustainable flow of energy.

In contrast, a thought that is unclear constantly changes its pattern, and it is unable to sustain itself long enough to materialize as a manifestation. Be aware of unclear thoughts. They sometimes create unfavorable conditions by mirroring a false image, which the mind attempts to project.

Also, the pattern of clear thoughts or images must be mentally developed and retained long enough to assemble sustained energy for a period. It descends, transitions into creation's atmosphere, and crystallizes into material form.

Intention is the energy that comes from your emotions. It is a powerful component, which sustains the kernel of a thought as it spirals into the formation of life. However, the intention may dissolve if the supporting energy is gone. As the magnetic fields of earth weaken, the energetic field of thought becomes increasingly strong, and less energy is required to carry the force for the duration. This can be the beginning of a remarkable blueprint for life, which is filled with peace, joy, and abundance.

There are two planes to consider when engaging in the creative process: *the heavenly plane* and *the earthly plane*. Both domains are parallel according to some eastern religious views. The earth plane is known as the part of the universe that provides tangible evidence to the natural senses (mainly seeing) and that gives meaning to life in an unexplainable way.

Oftentimes what is seen with the eyes is not what exists. This is called a divine paradox. While the universe is not, still, it is. In my opinion, the universe is a mental creation of God. Everything was created while in His incorporeal state (invisible), which is known as Elohim, Brahma, or ka (spirit) depending on one's religious affiliation.

The universe's corporeal state (visible) is a shadow of reality, but many view this state as their truest truth. However, truth for you might be your perception, a statement justified by an experience, or those things that are discernible to the five senses (empirical). Before drawing a conclusion prematurely, let us explore the two aspects of truth: absolute and relative.

Absolute truth is described as things as the mind of God knows them, whereas relative truth is things as the highest reason of man understands them. The universe is like an illusion. Some speak of the world as a passing cloud, which comes and goes as the element of temporal change. The finiteness is connected with the concept of the created universe when compared to the ideal of the Creator. In an absolute sense, anything that has a beginning and ending must be unreal. There is nothing real except for God, no matter what terms are being used to discuss the subject at hand.

Nonetheless, all creation operates within the elements of time and space, which may fluctuate from their authentic, original states when they are manifested in the earthly realm. It will give the seeker an advantage to have some degree of insight into the nature and inner workings of reality and its existence. That way, the seeker is better equipped to manifest the thing(s) that he or she desires. These things are provided by the universe.

Many perceive the universe as being real because of its appearance and the material matter that it projects, which the human senses recognize. However, its many forms of appearance are just reflections of what the absolute truth is—*the real* that unfolds in relative truth and *the unreal*. But it is only from this absolute truth that we live, move, and have our being.

3

Absolute truth is the source and substance of all existence. It arises from a space of nothingness, which has not been manifested. Relative truth is disguised in material form throughout the universe. In science and religion, absolute and relative truths are considered the two most powerful forces shaping today's society. From the perspective of relative truth, science strives to learn the mysteries of creation, whereas from an absolute perspective, religion seeks to know the Creator of mysteries. Such comparisons drove me to seek truth in a deeper way, extending beyond the material world.

While some turn to religion and science hoping to find the meaning of truth for themselves, many claims to have found the truth by way of their religious beliefs. These people may spend much of their time trying to convince others that what they believe is truth as well as their religion. Unfortunately, this false notion becomes confusing and presents a great challenge for the sincere seeker. It is hard to distinguish which religion, belief, or source of science is the correct one, when there are so many different ones to choose from.

However, no one particular person, group, or culture can claim that its religion or scientific belief is the right one. Truth is not measured by any religion or science, although many believe that truth can be extracted from both. If you are a person who only depends on these outside sources, you are looking for the easy way out—a shortcut. The reality is that you do not want to take responsibility for attaining the truth. Rather, you continue using your beliefs as a crutch so that you don't have to take responsibility for your own spiritual growth and development. Also, many people substitute schools, universities, and various organizations, believing that they have acquired it. Truth in its totality does not exist in such places.

However, truth will become apparent to a genuine seeker when this person turns inwardly toward his or her inner light and away from the outer world's dark forces. You must guard yourself from such an environment. Never accept the external influences of lies and negative appearances, which are presented via televisions, newspapers, or even radios.

The way to truth lies in your awareness of the Christ consciousness. It is not just a supposition or another concept, but it is a living reality within you. From this place of awareness, you are able to perform God's intentions for you: manifest in the earthly realm as did Jesus. He lived amazingly and simultaneously within the integrated realities of earthly (relative) and heavenly (absolute). Ultimately, He set the perfect pattern for humanity to follow, even though his loving action led Him to His death.

Because of this grand selfless act of Christ, many Christians claim that Jesus made all the necessary sacrifices at the cross—death, burial, and rebirth¾leaving nothing else for them to do but believe. His sacrifice requires more than just believing. It is a call to be an example to others but not to the degree that Jesus did.

Most belief systems are faulty and valueless. You can believe what you want and still remain the same, without achieving any fundamental changes in your life. Unfortunately, this sort of ignorance has a question mark attached to it. Truth is not a question, but it is a quest. It is not intellectual, but it is existential.

When faced with truth, a great amount of courage is needed to face it because it strips you of assigned identities, ideas, or thoughts that you have ascribed to. Furthermore, it causes you to abandon the things that you deemed to be true and real.

On the other hand, beliefs require no courage at all. They immediately vanish in the light of real truth. Truth is always present *within* and *without*. You cannot escape it. Belief systems of any kind are figments of the imagination. They make the believer think that truth is something other than what it really is. Consequently, you become increasingly susceptible to its false impression, as well as the illusionary nature of belief.

I know it becomes incredibly challenging to grasp such a concept, but deep inside you, there is a small voice that says to your heart, *what is being said might be true.* Your belief is a by-product of your cultural and social environment. It does not necessarily reflect truth.

The ideal of truth only exists in the essence of who you are. Your essence is God—divinity within humanity. According to Christian beliefs, man was created in the image and likeness of God. The terms *image* and *likeness* speak to His formless substance and not His form of appearance. This formless substance gives you the ability to create in the material world and to manifest the form. This may be a surprise to you. You may not have had someone in your life pointing to this creative power within you.

As a result, your ability remained hidden from you as you journeyed through life not realizing that you possessed the power to create your future experiences. When there is a lack of awareness regarding this innate creative power, you are more likely to create experiences or series of events that appear to be bad.

You may say to yourself, *why would I create something bad for myself? I only desire good.* Behind all appearances, neither good nor bad exists. To think otherwise is a false mental perception, which has formed by the undeveloped and untrained mind. This normally causes you to trick yourself so amazingly that you believe the lie. Not all that appears to be bad is bad. This pattern shows up in your relative experience to remind you of the person that you really are and the enormous power that is available to you.

But as soon as you believe the illusion of appearance, you actually relinquish your power as cocreator in the earthly realm. This makes you hostage to the thing, person, or event that you created.

If you wish to liberate yourself from the delusional entanglements of such bondage, you must look beyond the appearances of your experiences. When these patterns and appearances arise as things, people, or events, it is an opportunity to reclaim your power. When you reclaim your power, you can recreate an experience that promotes perfect health and abundant wealth. Remember, the things that take place in your life are designed to perfect your consciousness. All things work for the good of those who operate from the Christ consciousness that is within them.

As you abide in this consciousness, you will soon recognize that beliefs and systems are derivatives of thought. The very nature of thought is divisive and projects false images to your subconscious mind. It produces an attitude that says, *I am right in my perception, and you are wrong in yours.* Who can say that people are right or wrong because of what they perceive or believe? Communist countries believe that it is okay to rule its citizens by dictatorship. But does that make it right? Many would say, "Absolutely not." Again, what a person believes does not necessarily constitute truth.

Truth is a constant, does not change, and is independent of any belief systems, as opposed to belief systems that consistently change. For instance, some of the things that you believed as a child are no longer part of your beliefs today, such as the existence of Santa Claus and other imaginary characters. But truth has no limits or restrictions. It does not conform to any belief system. Although we think that our speech and beliefs hold truth in them, this is an incorrect assumption. Words, phrases, and sentences are not truth, and they cannot adequately define truth. However, they serve as a pointer and a conduit for truth.

There is no way to speak it. Words are only an echo of truth's reality, which seems to be a long way off, while what is unreal appears to be closer. This is the material world, with its false hope, false confidence, and false promises. What is unreal is a shadow of what is real and is preventing you from realizing absolute truth.

Truth is the essence of God's infinite nature. It dwells inside people, and it is manifested and expressed outwardly among humanity. Truth in its essence cannot be experienced, but it must be realized.

In my opinion, truth is a pathless existence that transcends the universe. The quest to know truth requires more than just head knowledge or gathering literary data from a book. It requires inner knowing. This knowing is intuitive, and it arises from the seat of the soul. Such knowing helps you discover and navigate the uncharted territory of truth. This undefined truth is encapsulated within the

Spirit, and it was uttered into existence as God's written Word, known as the Bible.

In the beginning was the Word and the Word was with God and the Word was God. The same was in the beginning with God. All things were made by him; and without him was not anything made that was made. (John 1:1–3)

In other words, the Word existed before the element of time and creation came into being. This Word (*rhema*) was and is a measure of the essence of God. All things in creation were fashioned by this Word. This infectious Word germinated within the soil of man's soul. As a fashioned vessel, you are manifested experientially in the earthly realm, for the purpose of self-discovery, and for duplication, and to create and express God's intention, purpose, and highest idea.

As God's creation, you have the best of both worlds: the nonphysical, spiritual world and the physical, material world. Divinity unites with humanity and makes you one with God. Your will becomes His will, your thoughts become His thoughts, your words become His words, and your actions become His actions. All is united in this state of consciousness.

I realize that truth cannot be taught, but rather, it is intuitively caught. However, spiritual principles are teachable, and they will lead you into the pathless space of truth. Jesus said, "I am the way, the truth and the life: No man cometh unto the Father, but by me" (John 14:6 KJV). Christ's personification served as the perfect pattern. It emanated truth in the form of spiritual principles. They exist in a place of authentic truth, which is in all of us.

Let us look deeper into the nature of its existence. In its purest state, truth is sufficient in and of itself, and it cannot be uttered. Truth is silence, and any attempt to speak it makes it a half-truth because it becomes compromised when verbally projected into the earthly realm. As a result, people often seek to know truth in physical things that are outside of themselves. But by directing your attention toward its roots of awareness and not its objects, one will discover the fundamental principle of being.

Truth is here and now. You are part of it, with nowhere to go. A person possesses a deep spirit of truth within, even if that individual is not aware of it.

When you are engaged in an intense moment of any activity, the deep silence exists. Truth surrounds you. It is in the air, stars, moon, trees, and leaves. It is even in the flow of the river and the dust of the earth.

But you go on ignoring what is apparent by continuing to ask the questions. "How can I attain it? Where is it? Is there a script for it?" Unfortunately, I cannot give you a meaningful answer, except in the elements of nature. Truth takes on many different forms, such as you and the pages of this book. God is truth, and He resides at the core of all forms of manifestation, which is often conveyed in silence. Only in silence, truth moves and flows in its purest state. In silence, truth is known and transferred.

Affirmation

Words, phrases, and sentences point to truth,
which is now unfolding within me.

CHAPTER 2

SELF-IDENTITY

———————————— •■• ————————————

Identity is the most sought-after aspect of an individual's character. Identity is searching for self-validation to substantiate one's own existence. Joyfulness, clarity of mind, and inner peace are available to everyone. It does not matter what existing conditions or issues are there. Turn the page, and you will discover the reason why. The grand question rests among the minds of many: *Who am I?*

Your identity is much more than your name or title. Identity extends beyond relationships, money, and possessions. Without using any previously mentioned reference points, do you know who you really are? I do not mean as a father, a mother, a son, a daughter, a Christian, or some other status. Who and what are you at your core? (not what you think or believe yourself to be) I am talking about knowing who you are beyond descriptions.

Most people do not have a clue, which often drives them to seek identity in other people, places, and things. These external projections portray a false sense of the essential self, which prevents them from discovering the inner qualities of their true being.

If you sincerely explore and investigate the functionality of your personality, you will potentially experience self-realization, as well as self-actualization. At this level, you will have only scratched the surface of your deeper self. You still won't fully know who you are or what lies beyond that. If what I am saying resonates with you, you might be able to change. Your identity must be something that you discover and not somebody else. However, some people have developed a high degree of self-realization, and they can help you better position yourself to begin your inner quest.

Your real identity is found beyond your current experiences, which are not authentic validations of who you are. Without the evolution of self-realization, you will just add more flawed ideas and concepts to what already exists in your mind. In order to understand who and what you really are, you must first empty your mind of all the mental garbage that you have unconsciously collected throughout the years. It is difficult to fill up a container that is already filled.

With its influences and conditioning, your conscious mind can serve as a barrier while you are on your journey to self-discovery. What you know can become an obstruction to real knowing. Your conscious mind wants to influence your subconscious mind and validate your own conscious beliefs. The subconscious has all the real answers. That is why the consciousness unconsciously imposes on the subconscious to extract the desired answers.

But because the conscious mind is already filled with what it thinks it already knows, which leaves room for nothing else, this is where the blockage lies, and it prevents real knowing from occurring. I am sure you already have a sense of self at the subconscious level, where the deeper self exists. The main reason why you do not know who you really are is that you have false notions of who you think you are.

Take a moment and think of a past, unique experience, even if it only lasted a few seconds¾a moment when things happened naturally and felt right. Suddenly, you experienced total calm and lost track of time, as if it did not exist. You were totally caught up in the present. This moment might have transpired while you were absorbing the elements of nature, taking a stroll through a forest or park, or lying under a tree and observing the twilight. It may have been when you gazed deeply into your soul mate's eyes and felt a connection on every level or saw a piece of stunning art. This striking moment may have been a breathtaking experience, where all was perfect and divine. During this short episode, all was as it should be, with little or no effort on your part.

Have you ever experienced such an incredible moment? During that explosive instant, who were you? In that flash, were you those things that you believed or thought yourself to be? The answer is no. These things did not trigger the moment, which might have been activities involving feelings in your body like sports and sex. While engaged in these activities, you probably were aware of intense stimulation, which produced a blissful sensation in your body.

However, your sense of self was not restricted to your body, although your body was present. While in this moment of splendor, you did not wonder, *Am I my body?* Your body was physically doing what it was designed for and as an expression of your consciousness, but it was not your identity. If you experienced a remarkable moment that did not involve your body, you were not mindful of its existence. In that instant, you were experiencing your true identity. Not all the things that I mentioned earlier were present in your consciousness.

For example, were you physically present? Did you really exist while you were in that state of ecstasy? You need to ask yourself these necessary questions when you are in search of your true identity. However, once that special moment passes, and time is no longer suspended, all relative things and events immediately reappear.

Again, you are none of the things you once thought you were— your thoughts, emotions, pessimistic feelings, lifestyle, gender, relationships, title, assets, beliefs, and ideas. They are not who you are.

I realize that this is a huge mental leap for you, as you try to understand the unfolding of your life experiences, which are seemingly real and true. In fact, they appear to be a large part of who you think you really are, but they are not. All happenings are only a reflected shadow, which is primarily designed to lead you to the true source of who you are.

By now, you may have concluded that you are something greater than what you initially perceived yourself to be. So, let us explore further into the nature of your existence, which ultimately leads to self-realization.

With much reservation, I will attempt to explain your true identity, although words, descriptions, and titles cannot adequately describe who you really are. Spiritually speaking, the absolute realization of who you are eliminates the *I* of the *me* construct of who you consider yourself to be. It vanishes and leaves no trace of validation or being anything or anybody. In other words, you become nothing but everything, as is God, who manifested Himself as the highest ideal into the earthly realm and in human form.

There is no need for validation of any kind because there is nothing to validate. There is no I, self, or me—nothing. Through absolute realization, you can know who you are, which is what you are not. This profound concept means that you exist in *everything* while in *nothing* at the same time, at all times, and even when you are engaged in the shade of your experiences.

To put it in simpler terms, you are a three-dimensional existence. This triad state is the totality of your being, which is personified in human form— the spirit, soul, and body. In other words, your identity is made of the three parts that encapsulate your person. The integration of these parts meshes as oneness with life. Metaphorically speaking, this is heaven, where real love, peace, joy, and happiness are experienced. If you choose to experience these celestial attributes, it is crucial that you find a way to be less dependent on your belief system and to not egocentrically defend it. This will allow the desired experience.

The more you identify with any part of your body, the more real that part causes you to believe that it is who you are. It is just a belief, and it does not qualify as absolutely real, although it is of a physical form. Thus, you do not need a belief or validation to experience your true identity, which is beyond spirit, soul, and body.

If you choose not to look beyond your experiences, you will not experience what *is*. You will not realize the experience of *becoming*. You will not experience being. Ultimately, you will not experience absolute reality. Consequently, you will only experience the effects of your beliefs, which are faulty in nature.

The question remains: *What can I do to gain access to my real identity?* Essentially, you do not need to do anything. Cease all mental and physical activities, get completely still, breathe, and simply be. That is what happened when you experienced that special moment of awe. The conscious part of you paused and just subsisted. You were fully present in the moment, without thoughts, ideas, or beliefs—really nothing at all. This very moment is registered in your superconscious mind, and it transcends time and space.

This state of being automatically relieves you of all negative thoughts, emotions, and feelings. At the same time, it allows you to accept people, places, and things as they are. Letting go is also a key to unlock the essence of your being, which you have experienced on many occasions while caught up in that special moment. You were not aware of it. This time, you execute it with conscious awareness.

The more you practice the way to exist in the moment by just being, the longer you can live out the pleasurable experiences that you have created for yourself. The most powerful application of any kind is to *be*, for lack of a better word. The more you expand, the more fulfilled you will be.

Affirmation

I consciously cease all notional thoughts, ideas,
and beliefs and give myself completely to this
moment, where my real identity exists.

CHAPTER 3

THE MEANING OF LIFE

—————————— •■• ——————————

What is the meaning of life? The meaning of life is inherent and permanent. It is embedded in nature, and every element bears its imprint. All things have meaning. This includes your life, even if you do not feel that it does. In fact, there is meaning within you right now as you are reading this. The meaning of life cannot be thought, believed, or experienced. It can only be realized. The meaning of life is realizing that you are in its incorporeal form. To put it another way, the meaning of life is the I am of God, which is who you really are.

If you attempt to think or believe your way into learning the meaning of life, you will miss it. Life becomes even more complex when you attempt to understand the meaning of life outside of authentic realization. Your attempt to gain increases your notion for need and want, which implies that you lack what you desire. As a result, you will create more need and want in your experience, as opposed to the thing that you desired.

Therefore, you might consider abandoning the notions of need and want. This does not mean that you cease to exist. It means that you have tapped into the fundamental nature of life and accepted all on life's terms. You are not required to do anything except to just be.

Take a tree for example. It does nothing. It does not uproot itself, move to another location, and replant itself. It remains in its original spot and serves according to its design. Nature performs only from its essence and in sync with the elements and seasons.

So just stop everything, be, inhale, and exhale. Become aware of how relaxing it feels. Notice that you are being. Do not think about it but inwardly observe it. Breathe in deeply, breathe out slowly, and just be. Repeat this until you sense inner stillness. You can execute this wherever you choose and at any time, but it is most effective when you are surrounded by nature. Inhale, exhale, and exist. Do not be anybody or anything. Be and simply exist. Inhale again and release it. Relax and let it out. Now tell me what the meaning of life is.

Affirmation

I now live from the essence of my being,
which is the meaning of life.

CHAPTER 4

TWO PLANES OF REALITY: HEAVENLY AND EARTHLY

—————————————— ●■● ——————————————

Reality exists on two planes: the heavenly plane and the earthly plane. Both domains are said to be parallel. The earth plane is the part of the universe that provides tangible evidence to the natural senses and gives meaning to living in an unexplainable way. All that the universe contains is considered real. The natural eye sees what is shaped by the mind's perceptions and facilitated through the five senses.

What is seen does not really exist. This is called a divine paradox—while the universe is not, it still is. In philosophy, reality is the state of things as they actually exist. It is not as it appears or is imagined. In a broader definition, reality includes everything that is and has been, whether or not it is observable or comprehensible. An even more expansive definition includes everything that has existed, presently exists, or will exist.

Ancient philosophers such as Aristotle and Plato identified a difference. On one side, you have thought that is parallel to the idea of reality. This is known as coherent abstraction: things that cannot be logically processed as thought. On the other side, existence is frequently limited exclusively to physical existence or something that has a direct source within it, as thoughts do in the brain. Reality is often contrasted with what is in the mind—imagination, delusions, and dreams—all of which are abstract.

Truth refers to what is real, while abstractness refers to what is not real (fiction is not real). The widespread theoretical worldview of reality would define it as one's perceptions, beliefs, and attitudes, which are directed toward reality, as in, "My reality is not your reality." This phrase is used as a conversational piece, signifying that both parties agree. It avoids conflict over the different conceptions of what is perceived to be real.

For example, in a religious discussion amongst friends, one might say, "After the great Judgment Day, it will be heaven or hell." The other might disagree, but in his or her reality, everyone will go to heaven. Reality is defined and interpreted by people's worldviews or within the conceptual construct of them. Reality is the totality of all existing things, structurally and conceptually and whether they are observable or not. They include past, present, and future events.

From a worldview as well as personal shared views, people often attempt to describe or perform mental mapping to extract certain ideas from psychology, philosophy, sociology, and other fields. These ideas shape many theories of reality. Ultimately, these people seek to validate their beliefs¾that there is no reality beyond their perceptions or beliefs pertaining to reality.

This perceptional attitude can be summarized in the following popular statements. "Perception is reality." "Life is how you perceive reality." Such nonpragmatic views suggest that there is no objective reality, whether explicitly verified or not. Many concepts that come via science and philosophy are often defined within the cultural and social fabric of life. Philosophy speaks to the different facets of reality, the nature of reality itself, and its link to the mind as well as the language and culture of reality.

Ontology is the study of being, and it is couched in terms of being, existence, what is, and reality as a whole. Ontology presents a description of the most-universal features of reality and the ways that they are interconnected. Ontology is a positive definition of reality.

A number of philosophers present and illustrate a distinction between reality and existence. In this day and time, many analytic philosophers avoid using the word *real* or *reality* while in dialog about ontological topics. The different views among the different philosophers seem to be concerned with only one idea: whether existence or reality is a property of objects.

In metaphysics and epistemology, philosophical discussions of reality often examine the ways in which reality is or is not in some way dependent upon mental and cultural factors, such as perceptions, beliefs, other mental states, religions, political arrangements, and unclear notions of a common cultural worldview. However, there is also the view that some reality is independent of any beliefs or perceptions. It is called realism.

Idealism's view is that the objects of perception are essentially ideas formulated in the mind. In this view, it is easy to conclude that reality is a mental construct created and coordinated by God.

Another view to consider is phenomenalism: the belief of a higher state of consciousness that exists beyond any mental activity. The mind itself is simply a compilation of perceptions, memories, and experiences.

There is an existing argument between philosophers that true knowledge of reality represents accurate statements and images of reality that correspond with the reality that they are attempting to represent. For example, the scientific method can validate that a statement is true based on evidential proof, such as the clouds in the sky. Others can point to their existence and believe that they will continue to be present, even though they do not watch or speak about them. This is another aspect of being.

Existence is often contrasted with essence (the question of what something is). Existence contains substance. Without it as the essence, it would seem empty and coupled with nothingness. Therefore, it poses a question regarding the world that we perceive around us: Is it the real world or an internally perceived replica that has been created by the mental faculties? From a philosophical perspective, the real world is an internal representation. It reflects a smaller virtual reality and replica of that world and our conscious experience, which is not of abstract objects, even though people will subjectively perceive themselves as existing in a physically real world.

From a universal perspective, realism can be viewed in two main forms: Platonic and Aristotelian. Platonic realism is the view that universals are real entities and that they exist independent of essentials. On the other hand, Aristotelian realism is the view that universals are real entities, but their existence is dependent on the essentials that exemplify them.

Affirmation

I consciously rise beyond my perceived reality, and I am unified with the essence of all existence.

CHAPTER 5

PERCEPTIONS OF REALITY

———————— ●■● ————————

Perceptions vary from person to person because some people see things differently than others do. You will always get different stories from different people regarding the same subject. As human beings, we have been mentally conditioned to automatically assign different meanings to the things that we perceive are reality. Depending on the circumstances, people will change their own perspectives or just make things mean something else to fit their views.

Normally, this occurs after observing the things that are perceived for an extended period. Wisdom lets you see that there is no fixed meaning to anything in life, even with its exceptions and assigned definitions. So, you can always change your perspective and the meaning of anything to fit your situation, if you choose to do so.

The psychologist and psychiatrist understand the perception paradigm. They make plenty of money by having you sit in a recliner and listen to yourself talk for forty minutes so that they can bill you for one hour.

The media, which is governed by the powers that be, has always played a major role in distorting our perception of reality so that we will conform to their global agenda. It is becoming more apparent that people of all ages are aspiring to meet the image that society is setting for them. For example, television commercials subliminally suggest that you can experience total happiness if you follow a proven program so that you will acquire the ideal weight, height, garment, house, car, and so forth. These are structurally designed to shape and appeal to your perception. Many are inspired by these appeals, especially when they validate who they perceive themselves to be. This type of validation makes them feel better about themselves and boosts their self-esteem.

Perceptions sometimes become a blind spot, preventing you from creating your own path to self-discovery and attainment. On the other hand, perception can be a feather in your cap, which helps you to focus on your path journey rather than on your destiny. In short if you change your story, you change your perception and finally, your life! The idea of change is a scary process for many because it sometimes requires leaving behind familiar people, places, or things, only to embark upon the unfamiliar and the uncertainty of what lies ahead.

Moving from the old to the new does not necessarily mean that you will lose anything. It means that everything is in your perception of it, and you have the power to adjust it. What controls your perception is your mental assessment of past decisions and experiences. It is all in the way that you deal with your perceived reality after processing the information.

If you become fixated on your perception and take ownership of it, you make it virtually impossible to rise above it. Perceptions are not the five senses, but they are perceived by the five senses. Your perception is usually shaped and formulated by the way that your brain has been conditioned and the chemical configuration of it. It includes your upbringing, experiences, social influences, and a host of other contributing factors.

There is no way to step outside of your experiences unless you let go of the way you have viewed your experiences. This can be a challenging process for anybody. You must do away with the perception of your reality (your perceived truth) because it makes you believe that you are your experiences. Even in this illusion, no one wants to be stripped of the things that they erroneously think will validate their existence, who they are, and what makes up their beings. Therefore, people unconsciously attach themselves to their experiences to find their identities. This is where the danger lies:

trying to mentally decipher what is real within the framework of perceived truth.

There are two aspects of perceived truth: relative and subjective. Both are a reality for many. They constantly change as one goes through the learning process of life. People can practice mental exercises to help them be more objective to certain viewpoints. However, if one wants to be objective about the things that one has learned in life, the shadows of experiences will be to no avail.

The real issue is people's inability to comprehend the intangible nature of reality and its unique existence, which cannot be experienced but can only be realized. It is like the wind. It cannot be traced, and there is no way to get a fix on it. It comes and goes from where you do not know. All you know is that it exists.

There are two types of reality regarding truth. The first is the physical aspect of reality, which is perceived as being objective truth. It is shared among individuals, linked to the five senses of the brain, and explored by science, which regards it as the study of the material world. The second aspect is subjective truth, which is causally related to the mind, personal thoughts, beliefs, knowledge, understanding, intentions, and experiences. These aspects of relative truth and subjective truth are abstract in nature. They are major conditioned aspects of humanity, which affect the world in very infectious ways.

Therefore, it is necessary to establish some a definition. This is especially true when it comes to philosophical ideas and ways that people view words in light of perceived reality. Even with the dictionary as a point of reference so that the definition and meaning of words can be located, it can be debatable and left open for personal interpretation. People's perceptions are distinctly different. As a result, they perceive something other than what is actually written in the dictionary, which is a sign of creativity. There are no rules against being creative because we give the meaning of perception to the reality that is associated with truth.

In nature, reality is objective. Perception is subjective to the person who is experiencing what he or she perceives as reality.

This meaning directly corresponds to the person's reaction. It is an anagram of creation, which forms his or her perception. There are creative individuals who anticipated this worldwide dilemma and created the dictionary to help people agree on the meaning of words, with the intent to minimize the negative impact on society means of interpretation.

Despite others' views, you are the one who interprets your perceived reality. You do this by giving a meaning to events and things that have happened to you. Again, different people can experience the same episode but have different views about what really happened. This is due to their past programming, which involves the five senses. Most people use these to decode different events in their lives, only to get a certain meaning.

However, you have the option to change the meaning, your reaction, or the senses that are actively engaged in your current experience. Eventually, you will change your perception, which changes the event you are encountering. You could simply give any meaning to your perceived reality of life, depending on what shade and lens of perception you are looking through: optimism or pessimism. For example, you may view a glass that contains a measurable amount of liquid as half empty or half full. You can fill it with different contrasting shades, tones, and colors of your liking. If you do not like a certain color, you can just change your lens of perception, which will reflect a change in the color.

On a subconscious level, you can apply this principle in any situation in life. You can alter your perceived reality so that you can experience a wonderful and desirable view of life, without any distortion. This perception is debatable on the premise of true life, and in today's society, it has become a coined term that says, "Your perception is your reality."

Living in today's society is living in relative reality. This involves interacting with and relating to others as a means of survival and success. Communication plays an important role in the scheme of perception because one must work in order to provide the basics of life: food, clothing, and shelter. Even if you chose to act independent of others, it would be impossible because all living existence is designed to be interwoven in the fabric of life. In other words, everything under the sun is interconnected, and you cannot unravel it.

At best, you can develop your own plan through your own lens of perception, which is appropriate for your lifestyle. Avoid becoming somebody else's plan, where other people's perceptions of you could dramatically shape your identity and self-esteem, whether it is correct or not.

The reactions of others sometimes affect you because they serve as a mirror of how you see yourself. What others say about you or your perception of what they think about you, which is usually the case for adolescents, is called peer pressure. As you get older, you will discover that being true to yourself is necessary to shape your own perception and the way that you view yourself and the world around you. You must understand that you cannot control or take ownership of the way that others perceive you. I often say, "What others think and say about me is none of my business."

Needless to say, most of us still have some degree of adolescence in us. Our self-worth is influenced by what others think and say about us. Normally, teenagers fall into this identity trap, wanting to meet a certain lustrous image or standard, which is imposed by others. Looking through this hazy reputation lens will sometimes cause you to achieve success by any means necessary, just to get the approval and praise of others so that they will see you in a successful light.

With great expectation, you crave more accolades that match your view of success. You interpret this as happiness, although success is measured by the standards of others rather than your own, which is short-lived. If you can avoid falling victim to this unclear perceptional lens of reputation, cling to your own definition of what success and happiness is, and aim for that, your life will be more fulfilling and pleasurable.

Most of our lives will be spent in the pursuit of goals rather than attainment. In fact, if you do not adjust the way that you view things in regard to your self-worth and reliance on other people's perception of you, it will eventually lead to psychological difficulties. When you depend too much on others for positive feedback, it places you in a very vulnerable position and creates an environment where others can control and manipulate you.

Therefore, strive to identify with wisdom. It will help you see clearly so that you can accept and appreciate yourself, even with flaws. Wisdom will assist and direct you in your personal journey, helping you to navigate through the maze of this hazy world.

Unclear perception occurs when biases are formulated from past experiences. For example, a people who have been raised in loving and supportive families generally have healthy and optimistic perceptions of themselves, other people, and the world around them. This opens their minds and creates a vibe that attracts the information needed for further growth, development, and success.

On the other hand, people who are raised in dysfunctional and abusive atmospheres may choose paths that lead them to further misery and self-destruction. They are pessimistic when perceiving themselves, others, and the world around them. They embrace misery over happiness, thinking that they rightfully deserve it. They become by-products of their environments and live as victims for their remaining days if they do not embrace the grace of God.

Perception is idolatrous because it consists of false images. They are not the real thing. Therefore, do not bow down before them as a slave does when coming before his or her master or as a subject of his or her king.

Affirmation

I now transcend the relativity of perception and its reality,
to awaken to the realization of my own creative soul.

CHAPTER 6

FULL ACCEPTANCE

●■●

Acceptance is a key factor in being in sync with the divine order of the universe. It serves as an antidote for life's problems and any negative emotions that you may feel. Acceptance frees you from the mental anguish and plaguing thoughts that invade your mind on a daily basis. The power of acceptance will prevent you from shifting, mentally and emotionally, between the contrasting spectrums of daily living. Ordinary life presents its own ups and downs.

For example, on better days when things are going your way, you are on the mountaintop. You are in motion, and you succeed at everything that you do. You have a hunch that pans out better than you had expected. Many positive things occur and make you feel as if the day was designed just for you. This kind of day makes you feel as if you could actually create a life that you would enjoy living. During this moment, life is like an exciting movie, and you get to write the script.

But when things are not to your liking and nothing happens as you would like it to, life becomes a struggle. You no longer feel like you are on top of the mountain. Instead, you feel like the mountain is on top of you. You have an overwhelming feeling of helplessness that seems to overshadow you and causes you to feel out of sorts and out of control.

It appears that you have no choices and that you are stuck between a rock and a hard place. It appears that you are under tremendous stress and pressure to deliver more than what you are capable of producing. You are often forced to do things that you don't want to do and to fight for something that you value in your unfavorable reality, which seems to beat you down.

There seems to be two realities or types of life that exist. In one sense, you are a victim. You have to take the hand that you were dealt and cope with it in the best way that you can, even though the odds are against you.

In the other sense, you get to design the day according to your liking. You become the producer, scriptwriter, director, and actor, all at the same time and while performing on the stage of life. That is a perceived reality. It is obvious which one is preferable. Which reality depicts life and the way it really is? Is there an acceptable answer to this question? Is it based on what you want to believe? I have concluded that the difference between favorable and unfavorable times is based on whether or not events are going your way. Whatever the outcome may be, acceptance neutralizes any one extreme and brings the balance that is needed to create harmony.

Three components comprise acceptance: acceptance itself, responsibility, and defenselessness. Acceptance simply means that you make a deliberate mental and verbal commitment to say, "Today, I will accept people, situations, circumstances, and events as they occur." This means that you know that the moment is as it should be because the whole universe is as it should be (divine order).

The moment that you are experiencing right now is the culmination of all moments. It is as it is because the entire universe is as it is. When you resist this moment, you are actually resisting the universe. Today, you can make the decision not to fight against the universe by not struggling against this moment. This means that your acceptance of this moment is most complete. You accept things as they are, not as you wish them to be. This is important to understand.

You can wish for things in the future to be different, but in this moment, it will be wise to accept things as they are so that you do not fall victim to your emotions. When you feel irritated, frustrated, or upset by a person or situation, remember that you are not reacting to that person or situation but to your feelings about that person or situation. They are your feelings, and your feelings are not someone else's fault. When you recognize and understand this completely, you are ready to take responsibility for the way that you feel, and you will make the necessary changes in all that you see as problems.

This leads us to the second component of acceptance: responsibility. Responsibility means not blaming anyone for your situation, including yourself. It means that with a creative response to the situation, you accept the circumstance, event, or problem as it is now.

All problems contain the seeds of opportunity. With this awareness, you can transform the unfavorable moment into a favorable one. Once you do this, every so-called upsetting situation becomes an opportunity to create something new and uplifting. Every so-called tormentor, tyrant, friend, or foe becomes your teacher as well as a steppingstone to heighten your self-awareness. If you choose to interpret reality in this way, you will have many teachers around you and opportunities to evolve.

Make it a habit to remind yourself that this moment is as it should be. Whatever relationships you attract into your life are precisely the ones you need in this very moment. Behind all events lie hidden meanings. This hidden meaning is serving your own evolution.

The third component is defenselessness: abandoning the need to convince or persuade others of your point of view. If you observe people, you will see that they spend the majority of their time defending their points of view. Defenselessness will allow you to gain access to enormous amounts of energy, which have previously been wasted. When you become defensive, blame others, and do not accept or surrender to the moment, your life meets resistance, and this will only increase.

You do not want to stand rigid like a tall oak tree, which cracks and collapses in the midst of a storm. Instead, you want to be flexible like a reed, which bends with the storm and survives.

It is wise to stop defending your point of view, especially when you have no point to defend. In doing so, you prevent the birth of an argument.

If you refrain from fighting and resisting, you will disarm all opposing forces and experience a spark of ecstasy throbbing throughout your being. This emotional state allows you to easily drop the terrible burden of resentment and hurtfulness that is associated with defensiveness. You become lighthearted and carefree. With certainty, you that know what you choose is available to you whenever you choose it because your preference comes from a level of contentment and not from a place of fear or anxiety.

Simply declare your intent through repeated affirmations, and you will experience the autonomy of joy, freedom, and fulfillment in every moment of your life. Make a commitment to follow the path of no resistance, just like electricity, which travels the path of least resistance. Nature's activities unfold spontaneously and without friction or effort on this path. Implementing the exquisite combination of all three components allows life to flow effortlessly.

If you remain open to all points of view, and you are not attached to any particular one, defensiveness immediately dissolves. Be mentally watchful and wait for the appropriate season when your requests will blossom and manifest into reality. This is the law of defenselessness. Mastering this process indicates that you have achieved a certain level of maturity, can make a deliberate commitment to be open–minded, and have a willingness to make major sacrifices.

The merging of these components is the ultimate driving force behind every great spiritual leader's triumphant achievement, enabling that person to intuitively lead and free the masses of people from the mental and physical bondage of capital control. For example, Dr. Martin Luther King was a civil rights leader who tenaciously exercised defenselessness at the hands of his adversary. He suffered physically, psychologically, and emotionally, but he did not retaliate.

Gandhi promoted peace and nonviolence, beginning in the Middle East and going throughout the world. Consequently, this served as a platform for conflict resolution and the freeing of the oppressed in India.

At any given moment, Gandhi and Dr. King were willing to die for the priceless causes of freedom and equality. Their extraordinary labors were performed through the amazing gift of acceptance and its associated components.

Affirmation

I now accept all things as they are, not as I wish them to be.

CHAPTER 7

TWO TYPES OF SPIRITUAL KNOWING

●■●

Direct knowing poses a fundamental question to the seeker, which is What is it? In this profound inquiry, the mystery of *knowing* unfolds. The unveiling of the intrinsic nature and the dynamics of knowing allow you to know yourself in a deeper way.

People are born into sin (ignorance). Ignorance is a darkness that blinds humans from perceiving God's light (higher consciousness). As a result, you drift through life without purpose, in a drunken state, and are confused and unaware. You have not yet awakened to the light of your essential being, which will illuminate your path of understanding. In this drunken state, you think that you are truly knowledgeable and have all the answers, but you do not. Failure is inevitable because you are missing the basics. You will remain ignorant and immersed in the depths of darkness. This form of ignorance validates not possessing any direct knowing.

Unless you know yourself, all other knowing is false, worthless, and shallow. You pretend to know, but you really do not. It is self-deception. You are fooling yourself. There is an ancient proverb that says, "He that thinketh he knows and knows not; to him be a fool, shun him, for he is not teachable. But he that knows that he knows not; to him be wise, embrace him, for he is teachable." – Confucius

Real knowing arises out of the evolution and transformation of your inner soul. It ascends to a higher altitude of change, which brings about an inward makeover. Direct knowing is different from regular knowledge. For instance, you may accumulate plenty of knowledge but remain the same. You can attend the greatest universities, achieve the highest degrees, learn from the most profound professors, do extensive research, perform intense study, and collect the most valuable information, but all will only exist in your head. It will be stored in your memory bank. You will discover that you are as ordinary and unaware as those who are mentally dull.

Much acquired knowledge will not alter the quality of your consciousness so that you can achieve authentic knowing. It makes no difference how much knowledge you have. It is important to understand that the dynamics of knowing and knowledge are different in nature.

Direct knowing is to understand innately, and it originates from inside of you. It is not learned, and it cannot be validated by anything that exists outside of you. Reversely, it is a state of consciousness (the light within you).

On the other hand, knowledge is an accumulation of compiled data or information that is continually passed down from external sources. Knowledge is learned. It often inflates the ego, fosters pride, and displays itself in the personality as knowing it all. Ego is a major stumbling block while steering toward authentic knowing.

A person of *real knowing* realizes that there is nothing to know, which causes the ego to vanish. How can you know? There is no way to earnestly know unless the Spirit of God reveals it through your highest consciousness. It is the most direct path that offers you access to such an illuminating place and where a small light starts burning within your inner being. You become most aware in your direct knowing when reality is no longer a mystery to you.

All of reality and its esoteric meaning are the by-products of God's power and creative Word, which is embedded in nature. God's attributes are similar to nature's attributes, but there is one slight difference. Nature implies the things that are not presently known but the things that will be known later. This has been proven over and over again by scientific research, which is knowable.

God is all-knowing. He is unknowable to those who seek to know Him in ways other than through the higher self. Even then he is indescribable.

Saint Paul stated, "For we now see through a glass darkly; but then face-to-face, now I know in part, but then shall I know even as also I'm known" (1 Corinthians 13:12). Attaining this state of conscious awareness requires the mindset that Paul illustrated in scripture, which gives you access to the throne of mysteries. So comparing it to the implication of nature, using the title or term God adds another dimension, that is to say, God is known, and more will be revealed.

Something more will always be revealed, but at the same time, there will always be the something that is unknowable. The mystery is infinite, and we are part of it. How can the fragmented parts know the whole? A person of real knowing understands the mystery, which is the great "I AM" (Matthew 13; 11–12). This mystery leaves you speechless. You cannot speak the truth because you can only speak things you know as a whole, and the essence of truth is never known in its totality.

You live, feel, experience, and ultimately, realize it. Mystery is always unfolding and linking to other mysteries. It is like moving from faith to faith and glory to glory. As each door opens, many more doors remain unopened. Doors of infinity give access to new doors. So who can express it? A person of real knowing will reply, "I don't know. I know only in part. I only know myself, and that is the highest ideal I can aspire to." The person of knowledge claims to know it all because he is ignorant. On the other hand, a true knower always admits not knowing, and that is a clear indication of real knowing.

It is important to understand that the moment you claim to know something, you immediately divide reality into a fragmented concept— the knower, and the thing that is known. People do this on a regular basis without ever being aware of what is actually taking place in that moment.

Allow me to say it another way. If you profess to know, God becomes three entities, and the one no longer exists. Again, knowledge is a derivative of thought. Thought divides, which makes God appear as if He is three entities as opposed to one. This is how the concept regarding the Trinity of God came to be. In absolute reality, there is only *one* existence; however, the moment you attempt to know it, the one changes into three, as I previously illustrated.

My aim is to emphasize that knowledge divides. That which divides cannot lead you to oneness of mind or direct knowing. Direct knowing unifies and eliminates the false notion of the knower, the one who knows, and what is known.

In direct knowing, you drop all beliefs, opinions, concepts, perceptions, boundaries, biases, differences, judgments, titles, labels, signs, symbols, and definitions. Consequently, you become nothing, meaning a *no thing*. In other words, you become equivalent to zero, and you are as undefined as true reality itself. This is the extraordinary reality and realization of direct knowing, which involves self-discovery.

In ancient times, "Know thyself," was inscribed over certain archways of temples and synagogues. Enshrined in this axiom is a mystery with a deeper meaning: To know yourself is to know God and the universe, for you are the micro within the macro cosmos.

Affirmation

I now enter the sacred chambers of direct knowing.

CHAPTER 8

THREE ASPECTS OF SELF

—————————— ●■● ——————————

There are three aspects of self. In order to penetrate deeper levels of human awareness, it is important to understand the threefold nature of human beings and the way the three aspects of their selves are intimately connected.

Three terms are used to describe the three categories of selves succinctly and simply: the basic self, the conscious self, and the high self. The basic self is the primary level of physical expression. Some examples are the initial cry of a newborn baby, a person's shout for help, or the faint whisper of a dying soul. All expressions originate from and move through the basic self. At this level, a human becomes aware of his or her surroundings. Some expressions of the five senses constituted in the primary functions of the basic self that includes laughter, speech, and other physical activities.

The basic self has its own instinctive behavior, which is distinct from the intuitive behavior of the high self. The basic self seeks sensations and stimulation, desires to control situations or other people, and just wants to be the center of attention. This aspect of self is ego-driven, and it constantly wants and demands things that often surpass basic needs, necessities, and inclinations. Typically, this behavior is seen in an individual who functions from the left hemisphere of the brain, which is known as the feminine aspect of the basic self.

If you put forth a real effort to understand this section of the book, you will discover how to contain the basic self and prevent it from overpowering the high self. The basic self is essential for balance and integrated with the other two modalities of expression. In fact, when total integration occurs among the three aspects of self, and you learn to control the basic self, it becomes your loyal and faithful servant.

You will develop patience, compassion, and understanding toward others and be genuinely concerned for their well-being. Moreover, your lifestyle becomes more organized and manageable, with little or no stress. Suddenly, your thoughts become more lucid, which has a direct impact on your awareness.

The conscious self is the home of your thoughts and attitude. It is the home of joy or sadness, as well as your ability to choose between the two. It is the domain of memory, idealism, and creativity. The conscious self is the bridge between the basic self and the high self. It combines your imprudent and instinctive aspects with your spiritual values. In other words, it is the connection between the right and left lobes of the brain.

When conflict of expression occurs between the two hemispheres, the conscious self becomes the unconscious self. The conscious self becomes deceitful, defensive, and evasive and assumes the role of a victim. If you allow the conscious self to fulfill its ultimate purpose, it becomes the grand appraiser. Consciousness translates spiritual awareness into physical consciousness and helps you to appropriately interpret altered states of consciousness. It is where knowledge, compassion, and wisdom are channeled from in a positive way.

The conscious self is fixed in the memory of the brain. It bypasses knowledge and connects with the present experience to create a storehouse of relevant information. When used positively, this depository becomes the basis of your confidence and self-esteem, allowing you to enhance your creativity.

The high self is comprised of spiritual values, philosophical ideas, and moral virtues. It is the seat of sensitivity and feeling. This aspect of your being identifies and decides your inherent needs. Being compassionate, creative, and spiritual are right-brained activities. Your highest form of expression is the love of God.

True love is a function of high self, whereas physical attraction deals with the basic self and mental conditioning of the conscious self. All three functions can display the attributes of love, but they are not love, in and of itself. Love's depth pervades every positive part of the human expression. Love is expressed through emotions, but it is not governed by emotions. The high self is best facilitated through the intuitive portion of your being, which leads to a profundity of personal freedom.

Affirmation

I now live and express the true essence of
my high self as God's ideal for me.

CHAPTER 9

THE COMPLEXITY OF THE BRAIN AND THE FUNCTIONS OF THE MIND

●■●

The brain is an extraordinarily complex organ that has many functions. It has the ability to reason, interpret, and analyze. It is the place where thoughts are formed and arranged so that intentions of the mind can be carried out. The brain is part of the central nervous system, and it is located in the skull. It controls a human being's mental processes and physical actions.

The brain, along with the spinal cord and network of nerves, controls the flow of information throughout the body, voluntary actions such as walking, reading, and talking, and involuntary reactions such as breathing and digestion. The human brain is a soft, shiny, grayish-white, mushroom-shaped structure. The brain of an average adult weighs about three pounds (1.4 kilograms). At birth, the average infant's brain weighs 13.7 ounces (390 grams). By age fifteen, it has nearly reached the full adult size of brain. The brain is protected by the skull and a three-layered membrane called the meninges.

The brain's surface is covered with many bright red arteries and bluish veins that penetrate internally. The four principal sections of the human brain are the brain stem, the diencephalon, the cerebrum (divided into two large cerebral hemispheres), and the cerebellum. Now that I have given a general definition and description of the brain, let us probe the function of this amazing organ—in particular, the formulation and facilitation of thought within the human mind.

The mind is not the brain. The brain can be seen physically, whereas the mind cannot. However, the mind is housed by the brain, and the mind is synonymous with thought. Thought is passive in nature, but thinking is more active and aggressive when processing internal data. Thinking demands continuous activity. For example, we change our minds, we make up our minds, or we are double minded about certain things. This perpetual cycle never ceases within the thinking mind.

What is the mind? It is a formless and functional continuum, which has the ability to perceive and understand objects on a mundane level. The mind is nonphysical by nature. It is not obstructed, limited, or restricted to the material world. The mind has common attributes that include but are not limited to perception, reason, memory, emotion, attention, and communication.

Another special attribute of the mind is that only the owner has access to its private sphere. Under normal circumstances, no one else can know your mind. They can only interpret what you consciously or unconsciously communicate with your words or actions.

Skilled and objective thinking is one major function of the mind, which requires the development of basic intellectual skills, abilities, and insights. Becoming a skilled thinker is like becoming a skilled boxer, ballet dancer, or pianist. To be an objective thinker, you must extend a network of interconnected mental traits. Maturing as a thinker is challenging, and it requires internal observation.

My aim in this chapter is to lay a foundation for better understanding of how the human mind functions. We will begin by further examination of human egocentricity and the barrier it represents. Afterward, we will explore several of the most basic characteristics that you can use to attain greater mental command or presence.

Your hidden egocentricity affirms itself through each of the basic functions of the mind. It is imperative that you understand those functions and the way that they work with each other. Only by understanding the way that mechanical functions of the mind operate can you acquire true understanding and transformation.

Observing egocentricity in your thoughts is one of the primary challenges that you will face while developing mentally is that your mind tends to think and feel egocentrically. Causing you to become deeply rooted in your own critical thoughts, troubles, desires, and feelings.

If you are not careful, you will seek immediate or long-term gratification based on a selfish viewpoint. You will not be concerned with whether your perceptions or implications are correct, although you may think they are. You will not be concerned with personal growth, insight, or veracity. You will lack the personal drive to uncover your own prejudices, weaknesses, biases, and self-deceptions. Rather, you will seek to get what you desire despite the thoughts or feelings of others. You will justify yourself in your own indistinct mind.

Thinking in this fashion indicates that you possess little or no real insight into the nature of your own thinking and emotions. For example, you may unconsciously believe that it is possible to obtain knowledge without a great deal of thought, it is possible to comprehend something without putting forth intellectual energy, and creative thinking is a talent that one is born with and not a product of practice and hard work. As a result, it will be easy to avoid the responsibility of your own growth and development.

Unfortunately, many people fail to see things from another perspective. Much of their thinking is conventional and one-dimensional; however, egocentricity prevents them from identifying such a mindset. Concurrently, they create inner chains that enslave them mentally, which has a negative effect on their relationships, achievements, and happiness.

In order to rise beyond the egocentrism that you inherit at birth, you must drop the false notion that your present state of mind is perfect and make an assertive effort to develop explicit habits that will enable you to overcome these common hindrances. This can be achieved by watching your egocentric emotional responses as they occur and immediately restructuring the thinking that is feeding those emotions. You do not deny them.

For example, you want to see yourself as an ethical person. Yet through your egocentricity, you may behave in ways that are deliberately unethical, such as discarding pollutants in the environment and justifying it through rationalization. Because of your lack of awareness, you are not concerned with the ethical or unethical nature of your behavior. You may not even be cognizant that you are causing an unsafe environment because of your egocentric state of mind. This mindset keeps you engaged in a perpetual practice of polluting the environment without noticing the impact of your behavior on it.

We will revisit the idea of egocentricities later, but it would be wise for you to think about what egocentricity is and to check your thinking to see if it exists. In most cases, positive self-scrutiny will yield fruitful results. Although you may not consider yourself an egocentric person, the egocentric parts of you still exist. This is important to understand so that you will be able to deal with your mind.

One way to deal with your own egocentrism is to look the way that you have allowed your identity to be egocentrically formed. As I previously mentioned, we are all born into a culture, nation, and family. Our parents instill in us particular beliefs, especially as they pertain to family members, personal relationships, respect, religion, political views, marriage, upbringing, education, and life in general. Normally, you associate with those who have similar beliefs, which parents often encourage.

Belief systems make you a byproduct of their influences. Only through self-understanding will you be more than a byproduct and able to escape the influence of your belief systems. If you were trained to believe what you believe, such beliefs are prone to develop into part of your egocentric personality. When they do, it changes the way that you believe. For instance, we are all egocentric to some degree, but self-examination of our mindsets reveals that we unconsciously use egocentric standards to justify our beliefs. We claim, "It's true because we believe it." Generally, we do not say this aloud but only in our heads. We think that others are right when they agree with us and wrong when they do not.

Let us make it more personal. The way you respond to others indicates how much you egocentrically presume that you have an exclusive insight into the truth. When you say, "It's true because I believe it," your words signify that you egocentrically believe that the groups you belong to have an exceptional insight into the truth. Your family, friends, religion, organization, and your country are unique and superior.

When you say, "It's true because I want to believe it," your words tell that you are more willing to believe the things that match what you egocentrically wish to believe, even to the extent of irrationality. When say, "It's true because I have always believed it," your words demonstrate that you are eager to believe the things that correspond to the beliefs that you have long held in your head. You egocentrically suppose the correctness of your early beliefs.

By saying, "It's true because it is in my selfish interest to believe it," your words point to the fact that you are quick to believe the things that agree with your beliefs—what serves the self and promotes an increase in your position, power, and prosperity, even if it clashes with the moral principles that you claim to embrace.

If you consciously recognize these tendencies and intentionally and analytically seek to rise above them, you will be able to think with a balanced mind. This will give you clarity, which can further aid you in your mental development as a thinker. You will then learn how to partition your thoughts into two categories: thoughts that will promote your egocentric nature and thoughts that will help develop your mindset in a balanced way. To successfully do this, you must develop a certain type of awareness and become a student of your mind's functions, especially its disorderly imbalances.

Affirmation

I now master the functions of my mind so that I may
foster balance for further mental development.

CHAPTER 10

THE THREE BASIC AND DISTINCT FUNCTIONS OF THE MIND

—————————— ●■● ——————————

The mind has three basic, distinct functions: thinking, feeling, and wanting. Thinking creates meaning and interprets your observations and experiences. Your mind does the thinking for you. It sorts events into main categories and identifies patterns. It lets you know what is happening in your surroundings. The mind figures things out so that you can better understand situations in your life.

Feelings help you monitor or evaluate the meanings that are associated with your thoughts. They serve as a tracking device to pinpoint your present sponsoring thought. I realize that it is challenging to sift through certain emotions when you are encountering difficult times, especially when you have tried everything possible to change your situation but have experienced no success. Most people get discouraged, angry, bitter, or resentful because it seems as though all of their efforts have been in vain.

Regardless of your current circumstances, do not give up. Be steadfast and unmovable because you can create better conditions for yourself. Do not allow what appears to be a hopeless scenario prevent you from living a healthy and happy life. You are not what you feel, although feelings are part of your makeup and sensory system. It is important to gain control over your feelings so that you will not be controlled by them.

Avoid becoming a casualty of negative feelings. Do whatever is necessary to change your feelings to positive ones. In other words, be optimistic. Start by seeing the good in every bad situation. For example, there was once a woman who had three strands of hair on her head. Rather than complaining or feeling bad about it, she said with much humor, "I will braid it." The next day, she discovered that she only had two strands of hair, and with the same enthusiasm, she said, "I will part it." To her surprise on the third day, she only had one strand of hair. Without any change of attitude, she said, "I will lay it down like a ponytail." Finally, she awakened with no hair at all, and she replied with greater joy, "Now I won't have to worry about styling or fixing my hair ever again."

There is always somebody who is worse off than you are. But with some mental adjustments, you can obtain positive results from the worst conditions by simply changing your negative thoughts to positive ones, which produce good feelings. I am not saying that you should discard the way that you feel because your feelings are real to you. Embrace them but do not take ownership of them. Choose a sponsoring thought that will render desirable results.

Disturbing emotions often cloud your thinking and prevent you from making sound and rational decisions for yourself and others. They cause you to see from an obscure viewpoint—a place that is not clear.

In order to gain clarity, it is imperative to quiet the echoing thoughts that inundate your mind. This can be achieved through meditation, which will be discussed in later chapters. When you relinquish your emotions and properly control them, you will transcend what you are presently feeling. This eventually elevates you to a higher level of consciousness and ultimately frees you from any mental or physical attachments, such as negative people, places, and things.

Negative encounters usually stop you from flowing in a positive vibration. Most people demonstrate all types of behavior based upon how they feel. Oftentimes, this is displayed in their speech, actions, or facial expressions. The source of emotions is thought, and it automatically polarizes the content of emotions. Polarization causes a person to operate from two emotional extremes: positive and negative.

Feelings are similar to a thermostat, which determines the desired temperature depending on its settings. Feelings emit a vibration frequency that manifests the current thought, whether it is positive or negative. It is important to recognize the emotions that you are feeling so that you will transmit a positive signal into the universe and create a life of your choice.

Recognizing the feeling process is half the battle. Make sure that you are emitting a higher vibration that will serve both you and others for the highest good. Here is how to apply this prevailing process. When you feel negative emotions, identify the type of emotion that you are feeling. Your feelings can be altered by attuning them to a desirable emotion. This approach will help you appropriately match the thought with the corresponding feeling.

It is necessary to ask yourself if the emotion is positive or negative. Then you will be able to determine your emotion or state of mind. So, if your answer is negative, immediately initiate the appropriate actions to choose a favorable emotion. There is no right or wrong approach to this exercise. In time, you will be able to accurately target the feeling that you are experiencing and make the necessary mental adjustments.

Once you have identified your feeling, your next task is to trace the thought or thoughts that induce a matching feeling. If needed, make the necessary adjustments to attain positive thoughts or change negative ones. Sometimes speaking aloud to yourself or pondering your thoughts will help you recognize the present emotion. This process will help gradually boost your emotional vibration to a level of feeling better.

Be mindful that an improved feeling denotes that you have realized that there is resistance. At the same time, you are freeing yourself of that resistance. Electricity travels the path of least resistance. Negative emotions bring resistance, whereas positive emotions bring relief. The same principle applies to emotions. Positive thoughts, with their equivalent emotions, are more effective than negative thoughts and their equivalents.

Do not get discouraged if you fall victim to negative feelings. Repeat the process until you experience success. Be watching for emotional shifts as they pertain to thoughts and feelings. For instance, if you found a one-hundred-dollar bill, you would immediately think of the things you could accomplish with it, which would generate a good feeling or feelings of happiness. But if you lost the same one-hundred-dollar bill, your thoughts would immediately shift to disbelief, and your feelings would be disappointment and sadness. Both experiences demonstrate the direct effect that thought has on feelings.

Feelings often dictate what to think and how to feel based on the meaning that you assign to specific events in your life. The main emotions to watch for are anger, pain, and frustration because each is an expression of and is rooted in the fundamental energy of fear. You are greater than any fear. It is only a figment of your imagination and a small, fragmented portion of your mindset.

You, in your completeness, are of greater substance than any one fragment that stands alone. You are an expression of divine love. You are a thought that is generated from the higher consciousness of God's universal mind. He knows no dimensional boundaries, and He does not conform to polarity, duality, ego, or fear.

The gate that opens to your emotional center must be protected at all times. It is located in the solar plexus area of your body. From this nerve center, destructive feelings are registered and transferred into your subconscious mind. When you learn to control this center, you will master your emotions.

You are now mentally ready to start the creative process, which places you in a position to create your own atmosphere. Every positive thought is accompanied by feelings, and it generates transmitting vibrations, which attract matching frequencies in the material world. In the same way that the law of gravity consistently responds to the physical matter of our planet, without fail, the law of attraction responds to all vibrations. Whether positive or negative, every projected thought that is focused on the past, present, or future contains vibrations and has the power to attract.

This powerful attracting influence offers consistent results in response to corresponding signals. It is omnipotent, omnipresent, and omniscient. Make a conscious effort to govern your thoughts, monitor your feelings, and fashion your words so that you will be in alignment and sync with the universe. You will surely acquire your dreams. It is important to understand that *wanting* and its associated terms imply lack. This relative term is used throughout this book to provide understanding for the reader.

Wanting is synonymous with desire. It gives you the energy to act in a way that you desire and believe is possible. It tells us if something is worth the effort or if we should even waste our time on pursuing it. Humanity is consoled by the idea of desire, but it remains unfulfilled within.

Let us look at this idea from a religious perspective. Christians have often been told, "If you have not been able to fulfill your desires here on earth, later in heaven, you will reap great fruit of pleasure and gratification. Until then, continue to pray. That will be God's gift and reward to you for all of your prayers, faithfulness, obedience, and continual surrendering." Notice that by this statement, promises of rewards are projected into the future, leaving you to experience the nonfulfillment of your present desires. If desires cannot be fulfilled on earth, how can they be in the afterlife? This mindset has infiltrated the entire Christian arena. It is full of desires as well as projections for the future, which take us out of the present moment—the reality of God.

Is God not powerful enough to fulfill our desires? Is God not powerful enough to do something while we are alive, here, and now, rather than postponing it to the hereafter? God is a right-now presence. All things are perfect and present in Him, here and now.

Let us take a closer look at the nature of desire. It is necessary to observe the movement of desire because it is very subtle. Through accurate observation, you will see two things. First, you will see that in its very nature, desire is unfulfilling. Second, the moment you utterly understand that desire is unfulfilling, desire dissolves, and you become desire-less—that is, you enter a state of serenity and fulfillment. People will never experience personal fulfillment through the nature of desire, except when it arises from the true self. Nevertheless, it serves as a portal to the operation and mechanical functioning of the mind.

Once understanding emerges, desires vanish instantly and leave no trace or residue behind. When you are desire-less, you are fulfilled. It is not that the desire itself is fulfilled but that the transcending of desire unleashes fulfillment within.

On the other hand, nonreligious people will say, "You can fulfill your desire. Just struggle hard, gain the competitive edge, attain more wealth, prestige, and power, and succeed by any means necessary. Your desires will be fulfilled."

Desire cannot be fulfilling. The proof is evident in our constant appetite for external stimulations, such as experiences, achievements, and acquirements. The appetite of humankind is never satisfied, and it can never be. Therefore, desire will never be fulfilled because it is empty. Take a moment and ask yourself several questions. What is desire? Have I ever looked at my own desires? Do I understand the desiring mind? Have I encountered it? Have I ever taken the time to ponder and meditate on it? What is the true meaning of desire?

You desire a certain job. You search for it. You spend a great deal of time acquiring it. But is there any fulfillment? Once the job is yours, you suddenly feel a sense of emptiness even emptier than before. Immediately, your mind begins seeking something else to occupy it. You entertain thoughts of getting a better job or even establishing your own business. When you do, you feel that you have achieved your desire. Once again, you seek new adventures, and the feeling of emptiness returns.

This is the nature of desire. It always goes ahead of you. Desire always projects into the future. Desire is also hope. It cannot be fulfilled because its nature is to remain unfulfilled, and it is constantly peering into our future's existence. Desire is always on the horizon. You look at it, you move toward it, but you will never reach it. Wherever you journey, you will discover that the horizon has receded and the distance between you and the horizon remains exactly the same.

For example, if you have a million dollars, you then desire two million. If you have two million, you then desire four million. Desire keeps wanting more. Whatever you possess, desire always stays ahead of it. Do you get my point? How can you stop the rat race of chasing something that you will never catch—this thing called desire? It seems that your only solution is to abandon the erroneous ideal regarding wanting, desiring, and hoping, which prevents you from being in the present, where the reality of God exists.

This level of consciousness transports you through the threshold of God's spiritual domain, where all mysteries are revealed. Similar to Saint Paul experience, who ascended to the third heaven, spoke with tongues of men and angels, and had the gift of prophecy, which indicates that he understood all the mysteries of words and their meaning.

When you are caught up in higher dimensions of consciousness, you lack nothing. All notions of *need* disappear, and only God exists in His essence.

Biblically, the root words for wanting, desiring, and hoping were used in an ordinary context to reflect something deeper that allows the intrinsic nature of wisdom and understanding to emerge.

Most people drape their desire in a disguise that has a flavor of spirituality, which is deceptive. They often attend worship service and fast and pray for long periods so that people will think they are spiritual. Some go through the motions so that they can get something in return. People who are chasing after desires in this life are like a dog running after its own tail but never catching it.

You accumulate wealth, riches, houses, and land. Then here comes death, and all is left for others to squander.

So it would be wise to move toward something of higher order, beyond the material world, which will remain forever. It is important to pursue treasures that transfers with you when departing this world to a place where it cannot be stolen or taken away, not even by death (see Matthew 6:19–21). Nothing in this life can fulfill the desirable appetite of humanity except for awakening to his true nature where all remains perfect and complete without having a want.

There is an ongoing interactive relationship between thinking, feeling, and wanting. All are interconnected and inseparable, having direct influential impact on one another. It is crucial for you to understand the dynamics of thinking and their functions so that you can appropriately facilitate thought. When this understanding is properly applied, it allows you to mentally tap into the essence of your nature and release the creative talents within.

This inner force will literally transform your entire being. It will change the way you think, feel, talk, and act. Ultimately, you will harvest love, joy, and peace. You will be able to create your own experience in the material world and achieve perfect health, wealth, happiness, and wholesome relationships. This mindset is attainable. However, mastering and developing the mind can be achieved only through devout training and years of daily practicing watchfulness.

Affirmation

In this very moment, I now live from the riches of my being and not from the desire and appetite of my soul (mind).

CHAPTER 11

TIME AND SPACE

———————————— •■• ————————————

Time and space exist as part of the human mind, although objects relatively exist outside of the mind and within the framework of duality. Both *time* and *space* are perceived notions, which are orchestrated by the mind and described as illusions. However, many people believe that time and space allow one to comprehend and make sense of an experience for a certain period. Neither space nor time are of any substance or learned by experience. Both are elements of a methodical scaffolding, which we use to structure our experience.

Spatial measurements are used to measure how far apart objects are. Temporal measurements are used to quantitatively compare the interval between events or the duration of them. Space and time are transcendentally an ideal in this sense. The reality of time linked to metaphysical theories of time can differ in its descriptions of reality regarding the past, present, and future.

Present persuasion holds the view that the past and future are unreal and that only an ever-changing present is real. Externalism holds that past, present, and future are all real, but the passage of time is an illusion. It is said to have had a scientific source found in the law of relativity—concepts of process and evolution under the banner of time and space.

Another occurrence plays a role in the element of time and space. Phenomenology is a reality that is on a greater subjective plane and a personal experience and interpretation of events that shapes reality, as seen and internalized by one human being. Even though others may sense this type of realism, it can be an exclusive encounter for one. It may never be experienced or agreed upon by anybody else. This kind of spiritual occurrence only transpires on this level of reality as it pertains to phenomenology.

Accordantly to the webster dictionary, the word *phenomenology* derives from the Greek word *phenomenon*— means "that which appears," and *logos*— means "study." The phenomenological approach is designed to hurl you beyond viewpoints and appearances that are associated with time and space. Ultimately, it creates a balancing system to help you bring equilibrium to the spectrums of life's opposites.

Affirmation

I presently escape and transcend the illusion of time and space so that I can enter the phenomenological realm of reality. All is here and now. Here and now is all that is.

CHAPTER 12

UNIVERSAL LAWS AND PRINCIPLES

●■●

Universal laws are necessary for governing life and its activities, including the seen and unseen. Cause and effect play a major role in the universe, that is, it orchestrates the concept of balance within earth and creation. Universal activities such as life and the functions beyond life are only operative when laws are in place to govern them. Like all ideas, this concept is a theory that we know only in part.

These laws are no more factual or fictional than the myths of creation and the way that universe came to be, which is recorded in the Bible and rests in the belief and perception of Christian people. However, truth rests in the inner knowing of the center of your being, where God reveals His veiled mysteries. But before we can examine the concept of universal laws, we must first understand what universal laws are and how they relate to the earth and life.

Universal laws are the governing force that establish equilibrium between order and chaos, which both exist simultaneously. This is how balance is created within the universe. What are universal laws? In my opinion, universal laws were created along with Creation, whether we are aware of them or not. The principles of these existing laws have no exceptions, except for the law of grace.

When people do not understand the lawful workings of the universe, it creates imbalance in their lives as well as their affairs. These laws essentially rule nature, or more accurately stated, they are rules of the Divine Universe (the womb of phenomenon). Similar to the laws of science (gravity, relativity, etc.), the universal laws exist to give order to nature and its existence. Without that regulation and arrangement, we would have no purpose, no action in life, and no fundamental conception of wisdom or knowledge.

Principles that are enforced by universal laws provide order combined with chaos, which produces balance. There are theories that chaos existed before order was established in the universe and that the universe was born out of chaos. Thus, chaos is in all things. Genesis chapters 1 and 2 speak to this idea of chaos and order. In the modern Greek dictionary, chaos means "perfectness in creation." This consists of indestructible properties, energetic intelligence, atoms, and particles that do not have order.

Chaos is a measure of the essence of all things that have been made in the universe. It is the formless void of primitive substance. Some call it the big bang theory, but for many people, this concept is difficult to grasp, so let me illustrate it with examples.

Prior to your birth, you, working through your *essence,* created an outline (blueprint) of your embodied life. Like a navigator, you laid out the chartered path that you wished to journey and created situations and occurrences that caused you to remember your origin. You did this while undergoing certain experiences, which heightened your awareness and made you intent on being more enlightened. This is the *order* of your life.

On the other hand, chaos is personified through the mental state of your beingness. Which signifies that you have the free will to choose. But like a construction site, while you are building from that blueprint to construct a balanced life, circumstances may arise requiring you to make some other choices. This type of chaos brings balance to order.

Your free will and choice are the chaos in your life that meshes with order and brings total balance to your life. The balance helps you make the best choices and decisions for your spiritual growth and soul's evolution.

Some people believe that life is not preordained, and that free will and choices are what create chaos, as their decisions determine their outcomes. This particular notion falls under the governing law of cause and effect. A law in which you can use to build a better and balanced life.

Affirmation

The combined forces of universal laws—order and chaos—bring balance to my life and cause me to remember who I am in the I Am.

CHAPTER 13

THE CONCEPT OF BALANCE

Everything that exists in the material world, both seen and unseen, is brought into balance by the universal laws so that equilibrium is fostered in creation and the elements in the universal plane. When you understand this simple principle, you will gain insight into the elaborate workings of the universe, as it pertains to balance in the law of duality (existence and nonexistence).

In addition, you will discover the intrinsic presence of balance. Yin and yang (a term from the Chinese culture) is another theory of existence that requires balance among opposite forces because of the very essence of their natures.

The original name for God is YAHWEH, which is derived from the tetragrammaton YHWH. It is a name so sacred that the holiest priests had no utterance for it. The vowels *A* and *E* have been included so that it would be pronounceable in the English language. When grammatically broken down, YAH means masculinity, and WEH means femininity.

Let me further illustrate. Adam was created with both male and female within him, reflecting the nature of God in image form. The woman Eve was personified within him. The man was christened with the title Adam (see Genesis 5:1–2). God caused Adam to fall into a deep state of unconsciousness and removed a rib from his side. He made the woman and presented her unto Adam (see Genesis 2:21–22).

This is where the universal law of balance kicked in. By extracting the letter, *A* from the name Adam and inserting it between the *YH* of the tetragrammaton, YAH, the masculine aspect of YAHWEH was formulated. In order to maintain balance, the vowel *E* was extracted from the name Eve and inserted between the *WH* of the tetragrammaton. This formulated WEH, the feminine aspect of YAHWEH, which made total equilibrium. In fact, the name confirms that both a masculine and feminine aspect exists in God's nature.

Vowels are placed in words to create a harmonic sound for proper pronunciation. The concept of nonexistence could not be without the concept of being. By the same token, the concept of being could not be without the concept of nonexistence. Upholding both concepts require balance. Without balance, only one concept would exist or not exist, and the result would be imbalance.

Time is an element in the scales of balance. It is a concept that allows our perceptions to rotate from being to not being and from the past into the future. This moment, which is all we truly ever experience, is like the swivel of a balance within the concept of time. Without time or the perception of it, we would not be able to hold onto the notion of opposites, as with yin and yang, good and evil, and existence and nonexistence. Although opposites appear to be separate, nevertheless, they are interdependent within the concept of time.

The idea of separation is a mirage. Things appear to oppose one another. This distorted perception produces an internal struggle, until balance is achieved by the merger of the opposing ideals. We often perpetuate this imprecise perception of distance and time, where all existence is in a recurring evolutionary process of improvement with destiny. During this process, the inaccurate timing of an event that points to destiny can sometimes be fatal but can be prevented through the law of acceptance and tolerance. These are the only tools that are available to prevent self-destruction.

The existence of opposites is exemplified by the pendulum of a clock. It is a symbol that represents time. It swings from left to right without fail. Through observation, one will discover that the pendulum can only be on the left or right at any given moment, except at that moment when it is precisely centered. Then it is not on the left or the right, but it is balanced in the center. Wow! Think of that moment when the pendulum is centered as the present moment in time when both spectrums of left and right exist simultaneously in the here and now. The concept of here and now orders our center of attention to the center of our existence. The pivot in time between all occurrences in past and future is where all creation resides in *balance*. The here and now is all that is, ever was, or ever will be.

Relatively so, it is only in the here and now that you can experience time without end through the realization of I Am. The here and now is truth in its simplest form. In the here and now, there is only I Am. No space exists for I was, or I will be. The illusion of time is at a standstill in the face of infinity, just like the pendulum at that crucial moment of balance between the ticktocks of time and the concepts of opposition. All things in creation coexist in the here and now.

At this point, the concepts of opposition become one. All things persist without the chimera of time and remain within the mutual and timeless state of balance. Similar to the words on this page, a complete script exists here and now, in spite of your perceived process of evolution and experience in time to read and comprehend it. It is important to point out that the equilibrium between the existence of the words and their nonexistence, which is revealed by the existence of the spaces between them, allows for your notion of separation and time in reading them. This principle of balance applies to living and not living; it is balanced between life and death and existence and nonexistence.

I came to realize how important it was to have a balanced life after I became familiar with this concept. When I started, it was a real challenge for me to strike balance within myself, let alone with things outside of me. I operated from both extremes of life's spectrum and constantly struggled to find a means of balance. As a result, I experienced emptiness and frustration. Imbalance affected every area of my life: spiritual, mental, and physical. It also affected my relationships and social and financial affairs.

Needless to say, everything in my life was in total disarray. Not until I contemplated the idea of balance did, I see the light. Things became clear: my spiritual understanding, thinking, and way of living. I was able to see the relationship between my activities and the events that were occurring in the universe around me. I understood how polarity existed in the spectrums of two extremes, which correlated with my life as a whole. This nullified the false perception of things being separate.

I have since modified my way of thinking and my practice of whole brain thinking (both hemispheres of the brain), as opposed to most people, who only think from one side of the brain. I was able to restructure my way of living, physically, mentally, financially. I began to eat healthier and exercised daily. I am now so grateful to realize and experience the divine gift of balance, which was provided by God through the universe.

My existence is in perfect balance. It was formed by energy, as a means to expand itself into matter, which is you and me. Balancing spiritual energy with physical matter was the very first act of balance (the creation in Genesis).

Nowadays, people are starting to take a closer look at themselves and their lives as they pertain to balance. They observe their interactions with family members, coworkers, and business affairs. They seek the right balance that is conducive for their everyday lifestyles, whether it is on a conscious or subconscious level.

Unfortunately, when it comes to spiritual dealings, most people back away because the common idea of what a spiritual person is can be far beyond their ability to achieve. They glance into a mental rearview mirror of guilt, criticizing themselves for doing something that they thought was unspiritual. Then they mentally beat themselves up about it. Usually, they repeat this vicious cycle.

It is important to remember that our incarnated beings and physicality's make up a percentage of who we really are. Therefore, it would be wise to bring as much balance as possible to the carnal and spiritual entities. There is a constant inner struggle to maintain balance between the two because we are driven by humanistic desires and emotions. There is no need to beat ourselves up about it, even though our human traits are not always in alignment with our spiritual thinking or customs.

Again, do not be too hard on yourself. It has been said that too much of a good thing can still be bad for you. Engaging too much in spiritual activity without balance is no better than living in the physical realm and never giving a thought to the spiritual. That is living in extremes and not living in balance. Many people possess a certain notion about being spiritual by not doing certain things: using profanity, lying, drinking alcohol, doing drugs, or wearing certain clothes that accentuate your shape.

I am not saying that some of the things are necessarily right or the best of human behavior. What I am saying is this: Measuring your spirituality by don'ts alone is not living in balance. The key is forming equilibrium between the dos and don'ts so that you can create a consistent harmonic flow in your thoughts, speech, actions, and behavior. Then you will experience the freedom of balance and not be led or driven by emotions, even though emotions are a necessary component within the human construct.

Human emotions help you better respond to personal situations in a positive manner and without reacting in a negative way. For example, if you emotionally strike out at the person who made you angry, you will have to face the penalty of the energy that you created by doing so. It is better to accept the emotion that you are feeling without prejudice, let it go, and allow the divine laws of karma to render justice.

If you act upon the emotion of anger to retaliate, you are no better off than the person who upset you. On the other hand, being spiritual means trusting in the Divine to center your being as you attune to a higher vibration of emotions. Be defenseless and let the divine forces of the universe deliver justice to those who honestly warrant it. The letting-go method will allow you to free yourself of all negative emotional baggage, such as anger, hurt, and hate.

Learn to master your emotions and move on with your life in balance. To some degree, we all have emotional issues to deal with, simply due to being human and spiritual beings in a relative sense. For that reason, it would be wise to accept those counterproductive traits that we notice in ourselves as unspiritual so that we can avoid inner conflict, with the understanding that they measure our makeup.

How can you disregard part of your composition? It would be advantageous to seek ways to enhance the part that you do not care for, with the intent of bringing balance. The bottom line is that you simply accept the emotion for what it is. When you learn how to accept the lesser quality of your human traits, you will realize that they are just as essential as the spiritual gifts that you seek to obtain. More importantly, you are here to rediscover yourself in totality through the realization of balance.

Affirmation

I am centered and balanced within my being. I am stabilized between the pillars of my spirit and soul.

CHAPTER 14

THINKING IN THE PAST

— ●■● —

Thinking in the past is like our what-if thoughts about the future. Our if-only thoughts about the past can rob us of peace and joy in the present. The words *past* and *future* are illusions, which involve time and space. The reader can use them as reference points as they follow along and maintain a certain understanding.

Paul exhorts us in Philippians 4:8, "Think on whatsoever things are true, whatsoever things are honest, whatsoever things are just, whatsoever things are pure, whatsoever things are lovely, whatsoever things are of good report." We are to forget the things that are behind us. The past is no more real than the future.

I can speak from experience that it is hard to break the habit of looking back at past events and regrets. I have thought, *if only I had done that differently, If only I had not done that*, or *If only that had not happened*.

It is imperative that we strive to focus on *now* and not project on the unborn tomorrow. This keeps you from reflecting on dead yesterday. Sometimes it is necessary to look in retrospect for the purpose of establishing a contrast between what you want and what you do not want. Reflecting on positive memories is another valid reason to look back. If you do it for any other reason, you are setting yourself up for doom.

The milestone of memory can work for you when it is viewed within the context of the present. All excellent gifts come from a now mentality, which creates many possibilities. No good thing is withheld from you, especially when you operate in the here and now and put yourself in proper alignment with God's divine will and universal order.

Many individuals have imprisoned themselves by their own negative thoughts of the past, which keep them from functioning to their full potential. People's greatest enemies are their thoughts of the past.

Remember, if your current affairs are negative, they are just the residue of wrong thinking in the past that is manifested in your present (now). You do yourself an injustice when you define yourself by your current affairs. Set yourself free. Start creating your present by altering your way of thinking in the here and now. Then you will enjoy and experience fulfillment beyond your wildest dreams. Let the universe do what it was designed to do. You will receive unlimited treasures, and to your surprise, you will discover everlasting freedom.

You do not have to be a victim of thoughts of your past, but rather, you can be an overcomer in the present. Many people struggle with thoughts of the past. Even after turning their lives over to God, they still experience some degree of haunting thoughts and make doubtful comments like, "If only I had become a Christian sooner, things would not be as they are," or, "I wish I had been a better father [or mother] to my children and a better spouse." The indwelling Spirit will turn you away from the if-only thoughts of your past and point you toward the sovereign God of your highest consciousness.

There are so many precious opportunities that you can partake of while residing in such consciousness. It will allow you to let go of past failures and to serve and sacrifice instead of being self-serving. After all, you are in control of your life and affairs. Use your past failures, misfortunes, and rocky experiences to create blessings for your present (now). You are not a lone ranger. You are not traveling this journey alone, because there are many who think as you and live in the past.

If-only thinking is what fosters feelings of regret, and it does not acknowledge the here and now. It becomes counterproductive. The past is gone. It is beyond retracting. Reality is what is happening in the moment. You must deal with that. If you look at the past without trusting that God was in your situation, you will continually condemn yourself to a life of regrets.

I had an opportunity to observe an unfortunate event that a close friend of mine went through. He experienced great loss regarding his well-paying job, home, automobile, and marriage. Even though it was beyond his control, perceivably, he wondered what had gone wrong and how he could have prevented the catastrophe.

These plaguing past thoughts paralyzed him emotionally and mentally, which held him hostage. This prevented him from moving forward into the realm of faith and trusting God for restoration of all that he had lost. The more he dwelled on the past, tried to piece things together in his mind, and make sense of it all, the worse things got.

But the moment he came to terms with his situation and accepted his current condition, all thoughts of the past vanished, and gratitude appeared. Consequently, all of this worked together for his higher good.

My point is this: Thinking in the present on what is true and real is far more powerful than if-only daydreaming. Rehashing the past is quite different from reflecting on positive things from the past. Remember, the past is of great value when you learn from your mistakes and recall them so that you can recreate your present. Sometimes it is appropriate to be retrospective and remember how, in your time of need, the God within delivered you and brought you through challenging times. The greatest lessons are taught in the desserts and valleys of life.

You can use Psalms 77:11 to meditate on when thoughts of your past seem overwhelming. "I shall remember the deeds of the Lord; surely I will remember God's faithfulness." I reiterate that it is okay to reflect on the positives of the past as an act of remembrance, which is quite different from the if-only mentality.

Affirmation

I now forget the past and embrace the
present and the here and now.

CHAPTER 15

THINKING IN THE FUTURE

●■●

Thinking in the future is a projection of thought that is measured by time and space. It causes the past and present to be absent. This state of mind is often rehearsed, demonstrated, and displayed in the things that people do and speak. One of the most famous questions, "What if?" This question can plant a seed of doubt and fear in your mind about the future.

Although the future is full of the unknown, you can move forward in the assurance of your faith and know that the Divine Spirit will lead and guide you into all truth. It delivers you from the grip of fear. Therefore, there is no need to probe the future with fear-posing questions like, "What if I lose my job?" "What if I become disabled?" "What if my marriage fails?" or "What if I lose my business?" Questions like these can easily fill your mind with defeating thoughts and keep you in the vicious what-if cycle. This will hinder you from accomplishing what you initially set out to do.

This was the case of another friend. He explained to me that he was fearful of having a recommended surgery because it would cause him to be incapacitated, leave him bedridden and unable to work, and prevent him from paying his bills. Plus, he did not know who would care for him during that time period. I shared with him the same things that I am sharing with you in this book. Eventually, he overcame the fear, and everything worked out in his favor.

If you want to be victorious over your fears, you cannot continue to worry about the future and the what-ifs. Future thinking is only a guess, it is not real, you need to make every effort to escape this kind of speculative thinking. Instead, give energy to other things like your health, spirituality, parenting, marriage, and finances. Do not focus on things that are not real or will never come to pass.

Being overly concerned about potential problems drains you of energy and joy, and it can impair your ability to see the situation at hand. Take each day one at a time. In its present state, today is real, and you are equipped and empowered to deal with what today holds. God is not asking you to look down the corridors of time in hopes that something will just happen. Do not permit your longing of the future to destroy the pleasure of the present. God will take care of you and make provisions for your day-to-day living. All that you think you need is already given in this moment.

This is called faith, and anything short it is called fear that often takes residence in the human mind induced and fostered by ego. The acronym for fear:

False
Evidence
Appearing
Real

This enemy is part of the ego. It gravitates toward and attracts events of lower vibrations to create negative situations in your life without your being consciously aware of its actions. For instance, ego interferes with personal relationships by causing you to be controlling, prideful, self-serving, confrontational, always right, and afraid of loss. Ego opposes the positive vibrations that exist in the mind and attempts to keep you in a state of fear.

Although you may encounter trials and tribulations, do not let fear enter your mind. Adversity is part of life, and we all have experienced it to some degree. Adversity is designed for your growth and development and to help you evolve to your highest consciousness. The Infinite One is omnipresent, meaning that He is always present in this moment. He promised to never leave or forsake you (see Hebrews 13:5). Once you accept the idea of His existence and realize fear is not real, you will discover His majestic presence, power, and love.

What-if questions fail to acknowledge the God of your higher consciousness. Therefore, you must remap your mind to create positive thoughts using your awareness as a mental compass to assist you in accurately navigating through the illusion of fear. The reorientation of positive thought fosters peace instead of worry and chaos.

Remember that the future is not real. The future exists only in wrong thinking. You may be asking, "Is it necessary to plan for the future?" Relatively speaking, it is necessary for you to plan for the future and set goals for yourself, but the key is not to worry about things that are happening. Trust your inner being for all affairs and events. Have confidence and assurance that the things that happen to you will be used by God for your purpose and higher good.

But when you do set goals and make plans, do it all in present tense and with the mindset that it has already been done. Make plans in the best way that you can and put the details in context of the present, and you will get your desired results. Use your energy for present thinking and deal with what is real in the here and now.

Affirmation

I now focus my full attention in this present moment
to avoid the illusion of an unborn tomorrow.

CHAPTER 16

THINKING IN THE PRESENT

—————— •■• ——————

Thinking in the present is being present in this moment. allowing you tap into a profound place where you enter the essence of your true being—the real you, the core you, and a place of realness. This place helps you to see what eyes have not seen, what ears have not heard, what has not entered into the heart of people, but what God has prepared for you (see Corinthians 9:10).

To be in the now suspends you in the present, which prevents you from jumping back and forth mentally between the extreme, false notions of past and future. Both will stop you from discovering who you are—the true you. Many people go from the cradle to the grave, never knowing their true selves. They frequently misconstrue who they are for what they do. For instance, a person may say, "I am a doctor [or a lawyer, dancer, musician, teacher, etc.]."

Well, I am going to keep it real by saying, "That's not who you are." That is what you do as a result of your inner aspirations and passions, but that is not the essence of your being. The sooner you realize the difference between the two, the sooner you will come to know your authentic self.

In ancient times, over the archway of certain spiritual temples, the words, "know thyself," were inscribed. To essentially know yourself is to know God because you are born in His image. God is Spirit, and He transcends time and space. That is the reality of the present, which is only God. There is no past or future. All is present in Him.

So when you understand this principle, you will experience real liberty, peace, joy, love, balance, wholeness, wealth, and perfect health. You can achieve this wonderful state of consciousness with here-and-now thinking. All that you and I have is this moment, the present, and the here and now!

To experience this, you must be attentive in the moment with 100 percent concentration and awareness. I am not suggesting that you monitor your every thought because that would drive you nuts but be aware and watchful of how you direct your thoughts and focus your attention. It is so easy to get caught up in the past or the future when you are not aware of the present moment. So be on guard! Think only on what is true and real in the present, even though this is not always easy to do.

Some people are forced to face reality because of their unmet expectations. They fail to improve, prepare for, or deal with their current circumstances, simply because they feel that it is not the way it was supposed to be. When you do not accept things in the moment and as they are, no progress or solution is possible. It does not matter how much you wish for reality to be different. Many times, you will not handle existing problems because of it.

I know many people who fail to face reality when it comes to their marriages, relationships, personal affairs, and conditions. They have fantasies, dreams, or false expectations about what life should be like, but their thoughts are quite different from their realities.

When reality kicks in and you see things for what they are, you can either accept or reject it. Here is a word to the wise: Accept what is real because that's when God can work for you. He oversees, and He has overseen every detail of your life—your singleness, marriage, family, job—and every situation on a daily basis.

Acceptance of the moment can help you overcome all the false expectations of life's affairs. Act on what is real today rather than resenting your present reality and idly waiting for fantasies to somehow materialize. Remember, you can create your own experience by thought, speech, and action. So whatever you desire your outcome to be is determined by what you think, say, and do in this moment. Your present is a direct result of past thoughts to include your speech, and actions.

The past is history, the future is mystery, and this moment is a gift— present. So whenever you move out of the present, ask yourself the following questions, which will usually bring you back into focus with the present moment.

Where are you? Here.

What time is it? Now.

Who are you? This present moment.

So live in this present moment; your gift!

Affirmation

I now live in the moment, as God unwraps the present of reality that is ever unfolding.

CHAPTER 17

FREE WILL AND CHOICES

●■●

Willpower versus Willingness

God gave souls free will. A will is having the ability to choose and allowing one to be used by influences. I think that it is the Creator's good-willed intention that all souls become intimate companions with Him through consciousness and not as slaves or mechanical robots.

He allows you the free will to make choices to create a life. I am speaking from a relative perspective. From an absolute perspective, choices do not exist. Choices are illusionary in nature when carried out in the earthly realm like past and future thinking.

Let us examine free will a little deeper, involving the act of relative choice. For example, if you spend time with someone you love, wouldn't it be important to know that the other person wants to be with you as well? If the love that you are demonstrating is not reciprocated, wouldn't that have an adverse effect on you? Normally, both parties want to know that the other is responding equally. You want the act of love from your partner to be of free choice and not forced or out of obligation.

Nobody wants to feel forced into anything that goes against the will, but rather, that person prefers to make his or her own decisions. All decisions made by choice are performed through free will, and they are influenced by the intent and purpose of the individual.

In order to carry out an intended purpose, you must execute free will of choice, governed by the intentions of your higher consciousness. With the mind, you can do many things; however, you cannot execute them all at the same time. This is where the will comes into play. It has the ability to choose and make choices that produce favorable conditions. When you are elevated in your consciousness and understand the dynamics of the mind, you will then be able to see your will at work in the things that capture your attention. This is your unconscious will. It is not consciously applied.

As a result, and to some degree, you lose your free will when you are not consciously aware of your beliefs, perceptions, and values. You make your choices without conscious deliberation. Habits that have been formed by the mind prevent the conscious mind from being creative. Habits will become the dictators of your will when you make decisions based on old choices.

To regain your will's freedom, you must become consciously aware of what you have been subconsciously choosing. Then you can choose anew. There is no power that is greater than your will except love. No force, addiction, hatred, or law of nature is stronger than your will is. The true will is the dynamic, propelling force of every soul. It has the free choice to select and direct its focus on the various patterns that the mind creates.

The path of attention is a wonderful place to watch the footprints of the human will, especially when it is active. You become more aware of your choices and more in tune with your reality. The will is the leading and active principle within your soul. The spirit dimension of the soul is pure authentic energy, which is free of all limited mental patterns and directions. The mind makes patterns out of energy while the will directs it.

The will provides the soul with its driving force for growth and development. Without the will, the mind's past patterns completely determine the manifestation of the spirit. When this active principle is dormant or hidden, your actions appear to be passive followers of habits or moods. The will helps you take the initiative. It prompts you to go in a particular direction and channels your energy into action.

Once your will is inactive, it becomes difficult to take the suitable action needed to mentally move toward any direction at all. In the absence of will, it is virtually impossible to initiate the intent of your mind on only your desires. You become stuck and wishful with good intentions, but you are unable to do anything creative.

The will that helps you identify undesirable thoughts and stops them midstream. Then you realize that you do not have to think along those lines. Mental patterns have a force of their own, and they will follow the inclination of the mind. The will causes the mind to do an about-face and steers it in a new direction.

Once it is active, your will has the ability to release you from the entrapment of a particular mental pattern. It can alter habits and behaviors. This part of your will frees you from past vices, which the mind has falsely created. While the patterns of the mind are ruled by the past, the will is directed toward the future. Again, the past and future do not really exist. There is only the here and now.

The mind knows patterns. The will knows objectives. While the mind may shift from one pattern to the next at any given time, the will holds fast to a particular pattern and preserves its position until the goal is accomplished. The mind becomes quickly bored with repetitious stimulation, but the will is patient to remain focused until it meets its objective. It distinguishes your individuality (your true self) from your fabricated personalities.

Much of your personality is learned by what you have read, seen, or heard, and it only represents the shallow surface of your being. During the course of a lifetime, you are presented with thousands of choices. However, each choice takes you down a different road on the journey of life. The conclusion of your choices is your individual path.

You may ask, "Among the patterns of the mind, how can I make the right choices that are beneficial to me?" The will guides the choices. The will can also direct the creative functioning of the mind. Once this part of the will has been awakened from its sleep state, it becomes a source of guidance for help and direction. Also, the will is the part of you that is willing to subject itself to influences and guides beyond the individual self. This activity of will opens you up to inherent energies that are contained in the gamut of ideals.

The will opposes the mind. When the conscious mind struggles to oppose or control the activity of the will, it produces an inner conflict called willpower. Willpower is the domain of the conscious mind, and it is a counterfeit will. Willpower is the creation of the conscious mind to make up for loss of contact with the true will. In other words, willpower is often what the conscious mind substitutes for the actual will, while only the conscious mind desires something.

It is important to observe the symptom and ask, "What is being expressed?" and "What purpose or need does it serve?" When the need is discovered, a better qualitative approach can be applied to meet that need. This course of action places the conscious mind in harmony with the authentic will. Both become one, which leads to better results. You tap into the inner will and experience an intuitive guide that serves as a prompter, initiator, and a source of guidance.

If the conscious mind is ruled by willpower, the source of guidance from the will is normally hidden behind a symptom like a certain type of laziness or doing things in direct opposition of willpower.

The voice of the will can speak only if the conscious mind is willing to relinquish its control. A small portion of your will originates from within your conscious mind. However, it can be made apparent only through honest self-observation, self-study, and self-evaluation. Adhering to your will's voice and surrendering to your true nature will lead you into spiritual bliss.

In order to be successful in this process, the conscious mind must let go of willpower and embrace the component of willingness. Willingness is the closest part of the conscious mind. It allows you to experience the will. Willingness appears to be different from the will, especially if things are measured as a standard by willpower. Willpower appears as strength while willingness appears as weakness.

There is strength in true will, but it is often confused with conscious willpower.

Willingness best describes the will of the conscious mind. When we say, "I am willing to do whatever it takes to ..." we are expressing authentic will. In essence, we are saying that our selection of direction or goal is emerging from a place of deep contemplation.

The compelling, qualitative force of the will leads one to believe that there is no choice in the matter except to carry out the original intent of the will, which gives a different feeling than willpower does. The action of willpower gives a certain feeling of putting forth effort in the overcoming of inner conflict, whereas the expression of will has more a feeling of peace accompanied by determination.

Using willpower requires you to constantly rule in its favor and yield to its temptation and impulses, whereas true will does not ask you to rule on its behalf. Most of us can distinguish between those times when we must constantly invoke willpower, even when true will is activated. From the standpoint of the conscious mind, an act of the will is sort of a voluntary surrender to a choice so that what follows is more like an involuntary going along with it.

Willingness is a voluntary act that leads to the involuntary compliance of the will. One does what one must do. Jesus, one of our greatest examples, was faced with death. He willingly surrendered His will to a higher will—the will of the Creator in higher consciousness (Matthew 26:39; Mark 14:36).

Affirmation

I now willingly and consciously surrender my will
to the higher will of my God consciousness.

CHAPTER 18

DECISION-MAKING

●■●

Decision-making requires wisdom. Wisdom is the capacity to see the ultimate consequences of an action while performing that action. Wisdom exists only in the domain of your higher consciousness (God). People's intellect alone can only make educated guesses. Their degree of success depends solely on how well they educate themselves on the facts pertaining to the issue.

In the decision-making process, there must be a certain conscious awareness present that differentiates between seeking facts and seeking wisdom. Facts come from the knowledge that wisdom is applied to. Wisdom gives a directive to that applied knowledge to validate the facts. Remember that wisdom is from God, and facts are from people.

Applying what you have learned in the absence of wisdom often leads to disaster. in the bible, it has been said in the book of James 1:5, "If any lack wisdom let him ask of God who gives all things liberally."

God's wisdom always plays a role in your life, be it governing your marriage, children, job, business, or daily affairs. His wisdom helps you make sound decisions regarding your life's matters and prevents you from wasting time deciding between options that causes you to be indecisive and to procrastinate.

However, both procrastination and indecisiveness can be substituted with assurance by following this reliable pattern. First, identify the real problem. Second, research and correlate all of the facts that relate to the problem, as thoroughly as time permits.

Third, turn the problem over to God and completely trust Him. He will show you the direction that will serve the best interests of everyone who will be affected by it. Fourth, wait for Him to impress clarity and direction on your consciousness. Fifth, develop a plan of action and implement it immediately.

The answer you are seeking sometimes comes instantly, depending on the facts at hand. Sometimes it comes later. Maybe no answer will come during the time that the decision has to be made. However, you must rely on God alone to be your source of guidance. There is no right or wrong answer in the spirit.

The place of making decisions is known as the crossroads of life. The crossroads of life has four directions that correspond to the geographic directions of Earth: north, east, west, and south, which spells NEWS. The four points of the crucifix cross encapsulate the idea of the gospel, which means go-spell and share the good news. The Christ consciousness is the center of those intersecting roads, and He meets you right where you are. He is ready and willing to render roadside assistance to aid you in interpreting the signs and symbols while you are journeying the mental crossroads of indecision.

The Universal Spirit is always speaking, especially to those who have come to this psychological junction in life. The Spirit of the God within provides what you need to know and manifests what is called the Word, which is personified by the Christ. The Word was, is, and will be forever. This Word is expressed in and by the universe so that man can consciously understand the universal God through natural means.

When the word *universe* is broken down, it displays the oneness and essence of God. Let me illustrate this. The prefix *uni* means *one*, and *verse* means *written script*. When joined together, you have *universe*, meaning *one written script*. The script is the Word, which was manifested in the flesh who was a written epistle, known and read by all men.

Jesus, as the leading principal, inspired His disciples to follow His example. The Christos (Christ consciousness) is omniscient (all knowing). Jesus already knows the solution and remedy, so when you attune to the indwelling Word, all difficult decisions are then easily made, and your direction becomes clear!

Affirmation

Within me, I possess the Christ capacity and potential to make sound decisions regarding life affairs.

CHAPTER 19

MEDITATION

———— •■• ————

Meditation is a deliberate practice of the will. This altered state of consciousness happens when you are intentionally willing to allow the mind to rest on a single focus. It is the practice of becoming mentally attuned to your ideal and the training ground for learning to set the self aside and give full attention to what is presently at hand. It is the intention to gaze at a thought in your mind from all angles by turning it so that you can observe it from different points of view until you understand it.

You would unquestionably get a clear picture of anything after such a close examination. As a beginner, you may experience the challenge of having to control your thoughts and pin them to a single focus. Starting is difficult, especially when the spontaneous flow of thoughts in your mind is stronger than your efforts. The drifting of an individual's attention reflects the activity of that individual's will.

In most cases, you use your will to make choices that express your individuality. It is important to understand that the will is not the same as willpower. Willpower alone cannot make your mind stay focused. So how can you achieve a single focus? Meditation itself will help in facilitating this process.

Simply get into a comfortable position (sitting or lying down). If you choose to sit, get a chair, and sit with your back straight and your hands and arms on both legs (if the chair does not have arms). Place both feet flat on the floor, tilt your head slightly forward, and tuck your chin into your chest. If lying down, position yourself on your back. Relax every muscle in your body. Start with the feet and work up to the head. Always assume a posture that will allow your body to balance itself so that you will not have to make any effort to remain in that position.

Close your eyes and sense your entire body. Make any necessary adjustments to your posture to get comfortable if you need to. While your eyes remain closed, take a deep breath, and hold it as long as you can. At this point, breathe at a consistent and slow pace. Focus on your breathing as the air comes and goes. You will feel your abdomen expand as your lungs fill with air. This cycle of breathing should remain slow and rhythmic.

While observing it, allow the breathing to happen by itself. This is what it means to set oneself aside without interfering with what is natural. Trust your breathing process. It can be quite comforting. Breathe in such a way that if a feather were placed in front of your nose, it would barely move. During this stage, it is natural for your mind to formulate thoughts regarding your breathing. The mind will naturally wander and think about other things. This type of drifting may occur several times; nevertheless, immediately return your attention to your breathing. This is simple meditation.

Remember, it is the practice of allowing yourself to maintain a focus on a positive thought while ignoring others. It is not an invitation for the subconscious to speak up. You are not required to stop your negative thoughts. There is a lesson here. Fighting a thought is next to impossible. If you fight it, the thought attacks more ferociously.

Do not fight your thoughts or say, "I won't think about that." Instead, say, "I will choose to think about this." Meditation is not attempting to stop thinking but practicing choosing to return one's attention back to the main ideal when other thoughts come to mind. Once you cease resisting, you can expand your awareness and direct your attention to ultimately surrender to the light of your consciousness.

Meditation consists of two simultaneous processes: paying attention to what is arising and surrendering by letting go of arising thoughts. This is how you remain free from mental snares.

Jesus demonstrated this technique on many occasions. He would often pull away from the crowd to pray in solitude (see Mark 6:46).

Meditation transforms your mental and emotional states, which allows you to replace personal willpower with spiritual willingness. This is an altered state of consciousness. You allow a particular pattern of the mind to become your reality.

The practice of meditation grounded in the absorption of your ideal will help you learn to master other states of consciousness and increase your sensitivity to awareness. It is the gateway to the hidden powers of your mind. Always begin and end with prayer. It must accompany meditation, as faith does with works.

Saint Paul understood this powerful act of meditation. He penned a letter to Timothy, giving specific instructions to "meditate upon these things; give thyself wholly to them: that thy profiting may appear to all" (1 Timothy 4:15). Take full advantage of this method and enjoy the many benefits that follow. Meditation is a wonderful endeavor when executed properly on a daily basis. It makes you feel light and brand new. It opens a new awareness in your consciousness.

This type of experience literally changes lives and causes one to live a more peaceful, joyful, and qualitative life. Try it and experience the awesome sensation of ecstasy that penetrates your being. The implementations of prayer and meditation are highly effective tools to consider. Both have been embraced and practiced in many traditional cultures throughout the world for centuries.

Meditation and prayer are similar in nature. They are derivatives of positive thought, as each involves the use of directed intent and transmits a frequency through positive thought. Both are achieved by the execution of specific techniques that are customized to a particular purpose. In each of these conditions, the person initiating prayer is requesting intervention from the Most High (God) regarding a circumstance that he or she has a sense of helplessness and a feeling of powerlessness.

Conventionally, you may have been trained to view yourself as creation, yet in the same breath, you may see yourself as superior to other existing creations in your surroundings. With this mindset, it is easy to entertain the notion that you are separate from all else, and in that separation, you are not aware of the interconnection of all existence.

The fundamental concept of oneness is strongly embraced by ancient mystery schools and some eastern religions. These people are persuaded that humans are part of all creation and not separate from it. Each person plays a significant role in the occurrences of life events within creation, and each is an essential component of creation. I am convinced that these primordial concepts are just as applicable today as they were thousands of years ago. Your existence is, has been, and always will be a part of all that you see.

This is the oneness of energetic patterns, which your thoughts have connected to all things. The experience of each individual affects the whole to some degree. Each situation or circumstance that you draw into your life is a result of the immensely powerful energy in force. In the mental activity of oneness, you can plant and cultivate the seed of unity, which is attained merely from patterns of thought. It is unified with feelings to channel energy most proficiently and with deliberate intent.

In this mental process, you become the creator of your own experience, which has a profound impact on events and all that resonates within you. You can expect this positive result when you acknowledge your oneness with creation. The methodologies of combining directed thought and prayer as a process is commonly known as meditation. This is considered an elevated form of mastery.

It is clear why meditation can be effective, although it is passive in nature. Meditation is designed to expand your awareness and direct attention so that ultimately, you will surrender to the light of your higher consciousness.

Affirmation

I now give my entire heart, soul, and mind to
God through meditation so that His will can
be perfected and manifested in my life.

CHAPTER 20

VISUALIZATION

Visualization is another method for using your imagination to create favorable conditions in life. This powerful technique involves the imagination and feelings. It continually focuses on the idea, the feeling, and mental pictures of things that you want to manifest. It gives positive energy to the process so that it can produce your reality. In other words, you will get what you imagined. You can achieve these results in every area of life: spiritual, mental, emotional, and physical.

You might visualize yourself with perfect health, wealth, wholesome relationships, or just peace and joy. Through much practice, you will discover the visualization techniques that work best for you. For example, let us say you are feeling unhappy with your current financial status. Life is relatively good, but some areas need improvement. You can start by visualizing the improvements that you desire and watching them manifest as you wish them to be. There is nothing strange or uncommon about creative visualization, which you use continually and whether or not you are aware of it.

This technique could be accompanied by meditation. While in a relaxed, quiet, and meditative state of mind, visualize and imagine prosperity. Imagine yourself with plenty of money, aiding victims of famine, homelessness, and disease. Try to create a feeling in yourself that this is possible. Experience it as if it were already happening. Repeat this exercise as often as you can (perhaps three times a day or whenever you think about it). Be sure that your desire and intention are clear.

Chances are that you will begin to notice changes taking place in your life very soon. It should be noted that this technique cannot be used to control the behavior of others or cause them to do something against their wills. The purpose of this exercise is to dissolve your internal doubts, bring divine harmony and self-realization, and allow others to manifest from their most positive being.

Study the principles, practice the techniques with an open mind, pray, and then judge for yourself whether they are useful to you. If so, continue your practice for more growth and development. The results can be astonishing. You will discover that the changes in yourself and your life are far beyond your wildest dreams. Using your imagination is phenomenal. It involves understanding and aligning yourself with the divine principles that govern the workings of the universe.

At first, this process may seem impossible because of a lack of understanding and an improper application. However, it can be achieved by executing the visualization exercises listed on next. If you have a certain way to relax and meditate, by all means, continue to use that method. Otherwise, you may use the technique previously mentioned in the chapter on meditation or adopt the method that I will describe now.

You can lie down in bed, but if you tend to fall asleep, it is best to sit up on the edge of the bed or in a chair in a comfortable position, with your spine straight and balanced. This helps the flow of energy. Whichever position you select, begin by relaxing every muscle in your body. Start counting down from ten to one slowly.

Create a clear idea, a mental picture, or a feeling of the object, situation, or event, exactly as you want it. Think of it only in the present tense and as already existing the way you want it to be. As you are focusing on what you are visualizing, support it with positive thoughts. More importantly, think of a pleasurable experience that will spark a great emotional feeling. This causes you to be in a creative state of mind.

When you are finished, open your eyes from your meditative mode and immediately thank God for your experience and all that you presently have. This demonstrates an attitude of gratitude, which should leave you feeling refreshed, renewed, and invigorated. Conclude with an affirmation of your choice by writing or speaking it. For example, you could say, "I am the creator of my experience," or, "I am now creating my life and affairs as I want them."

We admire people with vision. We don't applaud their eyesight but their imagination and ability to see what is not yet before their eyes. Such people trust those images in their minds, and they are directed by them. They create actual realities from what was first only imagined.

Beethoven only had his imagination to invent, compose, and polish his music after he became deaf. He never heard it played. Walt Disney created a cast of characters and the means to animate them. Einstein developed the theory of relativity by imaginary experiments. You are no different, so whatever you picture yourself doing or being, you can get positive results just as they did.

The sky is the limit. Nothing is universally denied, but rather, it is given in the most gracious way. You can create what you genuinely want, be it love, inner peace, fulfillment, or prosperity—whatever your heart desires. So learn how to use your imagination.

Affirmation

I now visualize and manifest the mental
image depicted in my mind.

CHAPTER 21

LAW OF MANIFESTATION

———————— •■• ————————

The law of manifestation falls within the structure of perception, and it is open for personal interpretation in any way that we choose to perceive it. Oftentimes, that is how we create—without being conscious of that very fact. We create what we desire and not what we require. So be careful what you ask for; you might just get it. This axiom has been proven true. It is simple to create, yet it might be difficult to deal with what you have created.

Manifesting in the material world is extremely easy, and it is something that we do on a continual basis, whether we do it consciously or unconsciously (Usually, it is the latter). We create moment by moment, using the thoughts that we entertain in our minds without being aware of what is actually taking place at that precise moment. As a sidebar, I need to say that it is more complicated to get others to conform to your mental imagery because their own wills and consciousness are involved.

So exactly what is the law of manifestation? In laymen's terms, thought is the creator, and it is responsible for all manifestations that form in the material world. These manifestations cannot come until the intent or thought is registered within the subconscious mind. Then the subconscious mind must absorb that thought and process it for further facilitation.

Einstein once stated, "Thought is energy; to create it, just use your imagination." This quote has become clear to many, and those who use it and understand the implications involving energy and imagination consider it accurate.

Creative visualization is one of many ways to mentally mold a manifestation. But merely daydreaming or gazing at twilight is not sufficient for creating. Visualization has its own process of creation: a simple intentional and deliberate act that brings a desire or need into manifestation. It is accomplished by constantly holding a mental image in your mind's eye, accompanied by a thought, feeling, and word of the same vibration. You will manifest the need or desire in the material world when this process is executed properly. Creating with the intent to manifest requires both mental and visual focus. This prevents mental obscurity, which fosters doubt.

The slightest skeptical notion can delay, alter, or even cancel out the manifestation process. Keep in mind that the divine universe is governed by balance, so if you can mentally visualize something that is occurring, you can also mentally visualize something that is not occurring. As a result, the two images will terminate each other leaving nothing to be imagined because of the imbalance.

It is okay to make mistakes, and you will. Just continue trying until you experience some degree of success. As you continue to practice on a daily basis with increased focus paired with positive feelings, the things imagined will appear in your experience. However, there is a negative side that exist as well. For example, I spent a couple of months in the Philippines, seeking to invest in a couple of major projects that I thought were affordable and that would be the best investments for me, despite the large sum of cash that was required.

With one week left before returning to the United States, I was excited. I immediately went online to check my savings account, to ensure that the appropriate amount of cash was available for the investment. I also wanted to withdraw some money for the remainder of my stay.

Needless to say, I was unable to access my account. I attempted several times but had no success. At that point, I thought that I might have keyed in the wrong password during my attempts. So I tried again for the fourth time, but this time, a security-alert message flashed across the screen: "Access denied for security purposes; call your local branch with any question or inquiries." Still, I was puzzled.

With a week left to go, I ran short on cash, and I had to borrow some money from a couple of friends until I left. Meanwhile, I tried to phone my local bank as well as the bank's headquarters, but it was to no avail. There was nothing more that I could do, so I decided to enjoy the rest of my stay.

Upon my arrival in the States, I went straight to my local branch to see what had actually prevented me from accessing my accounts. What I discovered caught me by total surprise. It was something that had never happened before, and it took every part of my spiritual being to contain myself.

After coming to some degree of calm, I found out that a collection agency had seized my account without warning for a ten-year period of back taxes. It was due to the fact that my former employer had only made partial deductions from my biweekly income. Plus, I was never given any notice that I owed taxes for the ten years. The collection agency had waited patiently for the right time before making their move, and they had scored big. There was nothing I could do to reverse the devastating outcome, but I tried to move forward with a positive attitude.

For about a month, I felt mentally and physically numb and mildly depressed. I did not know how I was going to keep a roof over my head and meet my monthly expenses. This valley experience was a pop-up designed to perfect and prepare me for greater possibilities and to elevate me mentally to higher grounds of consciousness.

This was a familiar place to me, which I involuntarily revisited from time to time and now attribute to my continual growth and development. Therefore, I was able to regroup and regain my composure without anyone detecting that anything was wrong. I immediately and mentally drew from previous experiences but more so from the realization of who I was. I started applying the principles that you are now reading about.

Suddenly out of nowhere, the idea dawned on me to resume my writing on a project that I had started in 2005 but had stopped for a period of two years. While picking up where I left off, I was challenged and compelled by my own writings to live what I was telling others to do. I then became more focused in my thoughts, intentions, emotions, and speech and pictured what I wanted to experience rather than wallowing in spilled milk. It was time for me to launch into the deep end and be the first partaker of my own medicine.

I began to visualize and imagine myself holding ten thousand dollars, paying my bills, buying different items, and sharing with those in need. I would literally go to bed with a dollar bill in my hand, rubbing it between my thumb and fingers until I went to sleep. I did this to create a feeling of actually having money while still imagining it to be ten thousand dollars.

I exercised these principles every day, throughout the day. Shortly thereafter, I noticed that checks began appearing in the mail from unexpected sources. They were in small increments¾just enough to pay one or two bills that were due. As time went on, the amount moved into the hundreds. This encouraged me to go further and into deeper waters. I made minor contractual business deals overseas and locally, as if I had the money in hand.

By this time, I was thoroughly convinced that all things were possible. So I started making plans for my book. I set deadlines for it to be released and attended to the pending business transactions that I previously mentioned, all of which would soon require payments. I absolutely had no clue where the money would come from.

Nonetheless, I continued to move forward. I went back and forth and negotiated between projects without wavering in my faith toward God and my ability to create and manifest the thing that I imagined. I was now into the seventh month of my manifesting process, and I had always had shelter, none of my utilities had been shut off at any time, and I had not missed any meals.

I humbly share with you that in the seventh month, the financial floodgates opened, and I received several checks: one for $1,700, another for $2,200, another for $5,200, and more, totaling over $10,000. This amazing experience was a direct result of using the visualization of my imagination, which allowed me to pay all of my current bills and 100 percent of my publishing fees for the book that is now in your hand.

I am absolutely thrilled and excited about how my dreams are unfolding right before my eyes! I have more to manifest so that I can repay friends who supported me through those challenging times. Above all, I attribute this remarkable outcome to the grace of God, who is no respecter of persons.

Therefore, grab the principles of manifestation by the horns until what you want takes form and appears in your experience. This is only one of the many incredible and memorable stories that have left an indelible mark on me.

Keep in mind that things you envision, and desire should be lucid, precise, and as detailed as possible so that the celestial energy builds and generates what you are attempting to manifest. The extra details you attach to your vision add more energy to it so that you will have a more rapid manifestation.

This impression is absorbed by the subconscious mind, and it is most effective when you mentally retain its pattern for a long time, allowing it to build up in the ether (heaven). Then it results in a manifestation. There is no limit when performing this procedure. It is at your discretion. You can repeat this process daily if you prefer to. Normally, manifestations will occur more rapidly if the process is executed immediately following meditation or while in an altered state of consciousness (Alpha). Then the subconscious mind is more willing and ready to receive the vision.

There are various methods for creating and projecting visualization for manifestation. You can use your imagination to depict something that represents your desire and send it into the universe to take form in the material world.

Here is an example. Following meditation, visualize what you desire; picture every detail as best you can. Speak to it aloud, using a matching affirmation while concentrating with focused attention on that single need. Visualize your super consciousness transferring the mental image into your subconscious. Continue holding the mental picture in your mind until you experience a feeling of peace, joy, assurance, and certainty. Repeatedly speak words of affirmation that confirm your wishes. Finally, end your meditation with an attitude of gratitude and as if you already have what you imagined and visualized. Watch it appear!

From personal experience, I strongly recommend that you use a journal to do some mind-mapping and record any personal experience involved in the creative process. But before starting, jot down what you desire and the means and methods of accomplishing it. Annotate every detail as you reflect on your visualization and the things that you felt. Record your activity while in that mode. When your desire physically appears¾and it will¾write down how it came to you and in what form. Now that your vision actually exists, remember to render a praise of thanksgiving to the Divine for assisting you in the process of manifestation.

Many people think that to spiritually create and manifest your desire is complex. There is nothing complex about energy and its state of existence in the world. It is something that we learned academically while attending school. It does not matter whether the creative process feels simple or difficult. You can create and manifest in your experience as long as you understand the law of manifestation.

Affirmation

I am the creator of my experiences; therefore,
I now manifest the life of my dreams.

CHAPTER 22

THREE TYPES OF DEVOTION

— •■• —

Personal Devotion, Worship, and Meditation

Devotion is viewed in two different ways: religiously and spiritually. Most people view devotion as a religious practice or a method that ultimately leads to a spiritual experience. Religion is a system where methods and practices are supposedly used to achieve spiritual awareness. From a spiritual perspective, devotion leads to spiritual awareness without any form of religious method. It allows you to achieve oneness with God within.

In the religious system, devotion is directed by affection, reverence, dedication, faithfulness, attentiveness, and respect for or to some object, person, spirit, or deity. Devotion may also be thought of as action, such as worshipping, praying, and making religious vows. Devotion is universal and a common phenomenon in all areas of the world. On a personal level, devotion is designed to make you more consciously aware of God's presence. Above all, it connects you with His essential nature. Through this spiritual link, you are unified with the Father through the Son. To put it another way, you become one with God through the Christ consciousness.

The atonement work of Christ gives you access to the very presence of the Creator. When you break down the word *atonement* with hyphens, it is *at-one-ment*. People's ultimate goal should be to become unified with their source: God in consciousness.

People often strive to connect with something higher than themselves, which prompts and drives them to begin a search for it. They are not clear about what they are looking for, so they seek it outside of themselves and in people, places, and things. People fail to realize that what they are seeking already exists inside of them, which is God, their higher self. He fills all the cracks, crevices, and empty places within a person. He always reserves a space for Himself in you.

When you acknowledge His inner presence, there is no need to reach outside of yourself to experience fulfillment. In this sacred place of dwelling, you will discover the sweet communion between the self and your inner being, as they engage in an unending fellowship of fulfillment. In your daily devotions, you will take pleasure in directing all affections toward Him and render your heart, mind, and soul ceaselessly to Him (see Matthew 22:37).

The fountain of gratitude springs forth from the depths of your soul, causing you to give praise and thanksgiving as homage to the God within you. This emotional charge will elevate you to another dimensional state of consciousness, a mental place where agape love exists. During this spiritual act of intimacy, the higher self gently whispers and summons the lower self to a tranquil place for union and away from all distraction.

When you adhere to the beckoning of your Inner Master and respond with a willing heart, the infinite mind and secrets of the dwelling God are revealed. Spending time with God in devotion helps you to disengage from the lower nature of activities and engage in a higher nature of consciousness. In other words, during devotion, you cease your worldly involvements and turn your attention wholly to heavenly affairs. When your focus is totally on the higher aspect of your being, you escape all distractions and connect with your essential self in a profound way.

Your present state of mind will direct your steps and tell you what to say, when to say it, and how to do it. This inner sanctuary is a sacred place where the dawning of revelation, illumination, and impartation occurs. All of these things are passed down to you from the higher self to help you carry out your designed purpose in the earth plane. Devotion is more than the clasping of hands, interlocking of fingers, and bowing at the knees, as commonly expressed among many religious organizations. It is the immersing of one's soul into the glorious divine.

Universally, there are three common types of religious practices: the many forms of prayer, worship, and meditation. Prayer is entreating, supplicating, adoring, or praising a deity in a disposition of devotional service or attentiveness. The attitude of the person who is rendering devotion must be right before prayer begins so that the prayer can be executed with a proper mental inclination and sincerity. In some denomination's, devotion is often followed by dramatic expressions such as shouting, crying, speaking in tongues, and singing hymns. These expressions articulate the inner thoughts and emotions of the devotees to the Divine.

The second form of religious practice is worship. This is a formal expression of homage, service, reverence, praise, or petition to God. It is closely related to or expressive of devotions. Worship is performed in temple and domestic settings, and it may be performed by individuals or large groups. The basic pattern of ritualistic actions denotes personal attendance upon and service of God by the worshiper(s). It is common in worship to make an offering to God, which again is often done in the spirit of devotion. Some forms of worship are primary occasions for devotees to collaboratively express their devotion to God.

Worship can be expressed in many different ways. It is direct communication as well as an act of intimacy between you and the Creator of your higher consciousness. Worship starts at the throne of your being and enters the courts of your soul so that you can experience the very nature of God. This state of consciousness will allow you to connect with God in a personal way. He is always waiting for the invitation that summons Him into your heart. The Creator takes pleasure in hearing from you. Your voice is like a melody to His ears. You melt His heart, as a child does his or her parent.

There is no certain posture to take or method to follow. Simply enter into worship with sincere praise. This is accomplished through deep concentration, along with channeling the proper amount of energy to raise your level of awareness. The higher the vibration that is emitted from your consciousness, the more the spiritual realm becomes a reality to you. It places you beyond the veil of all appearances and into the place where God's mysteries reside—the Holy of Holies.

From this domain, He speaks His will to you in a small, still voice. His words will soothe your soul like a piece of music that is played and that resonates with every fiber of your being. This breathtaking experience automatically gives the listener a truer encounter in worship than any ritual ceremony could ever offer. Ceremonial worship is a creation of the limited human mind. It is usually performed in a customary way like kneeling in prayer, singing songs, and reciting scriptures.

All of this is conducted in the name of worship, while the mind wanders the universe thinking about daily affairs and problems, such as family members, businesses, social involvements, love affairs, interests, and pastimes—everything except worshiping God. Many attend churches, synagogues, mosques, and temples to capture the worship experience. Many others congregate out of habit and for social reasons rather than for a burning passion to know God and worship Him.

God is not confined to a physical building or any other geographical location. He is omnipresent. Jesus said to the Samaritan woman while at Jacob's well,

"But the hour is coming, and now is when the true worshiper will worship the Father in spirit and in truth, for the Father seeketh such to worship him. God is Spirit and Truth, and those who worship Him must worship in spirit and truth" (John 4:23–24). According to this passage, God is Spirit and Truth, and in order to unify with Him, it must be through both spirit and truth.

You do not have to wait until the doors of the church are open. You can worship God anywhere and at any time. The kingdom of God is within you. I am not suggesting that you stop attending your place of fellowship and assembling with other believers, but it would be wise to assemble with the understanding of true worship and its purpose.

Remember, it does not matter what method or location is selected because your intent and the consciousness that is brought to the existing object makes worship true and real. It is important for you to understand that all methods, means, and ways serve as tools to help facilitate your transition from a lower state of consciousness to a higher one, where joy, bliss, and splendor dwell.

Those who have not awakened to a heightened level of consciousness can only relate to common things in life. Their most inspired moments are when they are fully immersed in pleasurable activities, such as partying, laughing, dancing, or just fantasizing about life. Though these experiences can be fun, they have no permanency about them. They are short-lived, and they have similar features. For example, if you form a positive mental focus on something, but you drift from your primary focus, the pleasure becomes impaired or lost. There is fretfulness as the individual self merges with the object of its focus. This notion is created by the five senses, and their experiences are constantly changing, which reduces your focus time to a short period of one hour max.

Sight, sound, and experience of this world are limited. Not all are real worship. However, in the sound of the Word, a divine melody of this world is created by producing sound vibrations in the atmosphere. The divine melody is created by the Word of God, and the sound is carried by the primal vibrations that sustain creation. External music is heard by the outer ear, whereas divine music is heard with the ear of the soul.

The soul has two basic internal faculties. First, it has the ability to hear with an inner ear. Second, it can see with an inner vision. The vibratory Word utters a divine light and brightness that this world cannot give. The light to which I am referring is a vibration of flowing energy, which reflects what is in the spirit of humans. The spirit will allow them to hear the pulsating Word as well as see it.

Most objects in the earth are seen by reflected light. At the core, light emanates from everything as an expression of its internal migration and movement. The creative power maintains its existence. The mystery of stillness allows you to listen to the sound and see the light of the Word. The soul becomes magnetically energized and united with the Word, elevating it to a higher dimension. This is known as the path of the Word. How to walk that path remains the greatest mystery of all times.

Jesus spoke to His disciples regarding the mysteries of the kingdom of heaven, saying, "It is given unto you to know the mysteries of the kingdom of heaven, but to them it has not been given" (Matthew 13:11). He also referred to the two internal faculties of seeing and hearing as He spoke to His disciples. "But blessed are your eyes for they see, and your ears for they hear, for assuredly, I say to you, that many prophets and righteous men desired to see what you see, and did not see it, and to hear what, and did not hear it" (Matthew 13:16–17). Many seek this experience through the senses of seeing and hearing in an external way while in worship mode, but they remain blind to this mystery.

According to scripture,

Eye have not seen, nor ear heard, neither have it entered into the heart of man, the things which God has revealed them unto us by his spirit; for the Spirit searches all things, yea, the deep things of God. For what man knows of the things of man, save the spirit of man which is in him; even so the things of God know no man, but the Spirit of God; Now, we have received not the spirit of the world, but the Spirit which is of God that we might know the things are freely given to us of God. (1 Corinthians 2:9–12)

Paul is talking about spiritual things that are only seen and heard in the spiritual realm. The undeveloped eyes and the untrained ears of the body cannot see or hear the things of the spiritual realm. It is impossible to naturally comprehend or even ascertain the things in that realm, not to mention sight and sounds. In order to enter such a domain, you must experience an altered state of consciousness, which usually leaves you speechless.

While in this state, the hidden and deep things of God are revealed to you in the most profound way. You will have access to spiritual information about people, places, and things through the word of knowledge or the word of wisdom.

Meditation is the third type of religious practice where devotion is expressed. Many kinds of meditation do not involve devotion, but meditative techniques may be used. Meditation usually involves disciplining the mind so that it can focus on something without being distracted by frivolous thoughts or bodily needs and discomforts. For many practitioners, the goal is to achieve or maintain attentiveness to God. Meditation is used to perfect, deepen, sharpen, or enhance devotion. In such cases, meditation and devotion are synonymous with a calm and quiet heart and mind.

One particularly common meditative technique used to express, engender, or enhance devotion is the repetition God's name or rendering a short prayer to Him. The idea of devotion represents a person's natural inclination toward God.

All creation was brought into being to discover the indwelling Creator. Every species in existence praises God in its own special way. Even nature celebrates the Creator in some way: the dashing winds, the swaying of branches and their dangling leaves, the rising sun, and the tossing waves of the sea. This is the awesome imprint of consciousness that is embedded at the core of all existence, including nature, which sets it in motion, singing and dancing in ecstatic praise.

In this very moment, you can embark on an intoxicating experience when you direct all of your adoration toward your higher self. There is nothing more fulfilling than consciously existing in this state of mind, even while performing the most mundane acts in everyday living. The most perfect form of devotion to the Divine is when you become an instrumental conduit who performs charitable service to fellow human beings.

It starts with an inner surrender of your heart, mind, and soul to the higher aspect of your being. Many religious-orientated people try to impress others by their outward religious expressions, but Jesus warned His disciples against this behavior. He instructed them not to render devotion that could be seen by others, as the hypocrites did in the synagogues and streets, but to rather do it in secret, where the inner God sees in secret and rewards openly.

From the instruction of Jesus, we can safely conclude that He demanded that His disciples go into a secluded area for a time of prayer, concentration, and meditation. These various methods of devotion were and are presently considered to be a sacred inward act toward the God within, to demonstrate gratitude by inner silence or outward gestures.

Devotion is a powerful component, which will elevate you above perceived limitations, struggles, and hardships of life into the abundance of a world of freedom. Sincere devotion divinely propels you into the temple of your super consciousness, where God sits calmly governing the polarities of the negative and positive pillars that exist between the lower and upper regions of your mind. When equilibrium occurs among the two poles, a radiant light, which is generated from the act of devoutness, will illuminate your temple, and cause an outer glow.

Moses visited God on top of Mount Sinai. Afterward, a great shine radiated from his face, so much that the people could not look at him. He draped his face with a veil when he was with the people, but when entering the presence of God, he pulled the veil back.

The more time you spend before God, the more transparent you become before Him. All hidden things are exposed and made known. This is the place where God washes you clean with His divine grace and mercy. He showers you with His love and sanitizes your very soul. You are made anew to do new things, to live in a new way, to think with a new mind, to talk a positive language, to see with a new vision, and to perform great exploits. Ultimately, you will gain inner peace, poise, power, wisdom, and love. These are some rewards and benefits to those who make the necessary sacrifices of devoting themselves to such an isolated endeavor.

Many resist the idea of solitude because it cuts them off from the activity of the world—a place you become dependent on as well as complacent in. You may be quite convinced that solitude is something that you need; however, the enemies of doubt and resistance often flare up right at the moment you decide to engage. Unfortunately, no matter how well you plan and prepare for such a moment, the negative pillar of your mind rises to keep you bound to the lower nature of your being.

It is possible to break through the barrier of opposition and move into a position of solitude without developing a fear of not being in control. Ego convinces the notional self that you will lose out and that your ideas, plans, and dreams will be sabotaged if you are not in control. The reality is that God is in control, and you must take a leap of faith and delve into the unknown. Outside of fear, you take a risk by saying, "Here I am with my whole heart, soul, mind, and body. I am here, ready, and willing to move more deeply into a relationship with God. I make myself available and vulnerable by putting my heart on the line for the unfamiliar."

Your undivided attention is needed so that your higher self can direct your lower self into deeper devotion. While in devotion, you cease to fight against the reality of your condition. You accept it as it should be and not the way you wish it to be.

Do away with the notion of controlling the outcome of your past efforts. Realize that they are beyond your control. As challenging as it may seem, let go of all mental attachments and fragmented images of yourself, which you have allowed to define you. All false appearances are constructed by the ego to create fear. The ego frantically tries to maintain its grip of control, especially when habits and addictions are threatened, which can be very painful for the individual who has not yet evolved to higher consciousness.

Unfortunately, people use these kinds of experiences to further validate their existences. You are not your experiences. You are the epitome of inspirational splendor and much more that is beyond description. You will endure such experiences, which were initially created by erroneous thoughts.

Devotion sheds light on the false identities and dark areas of your life so that you can begin to see yourself and events as they really are. This enlightened state gives you the opportunity to learn and master yourself. The highest attainment for a person is self-mastery. To achieve such a goal, you must be driven by a deep passion and have an inward thirst and panting of the soul. It is a constant state of bowing inwardly before the higher self with a renewed mind.

In consciousness, you become a sanctuary for God's dwelling Spirit. His Spirit infuses your spirit, which makes you one with Him. Here, an intimate communion begins. The Bible says, "Know ye not that ye are the temple of God, and that the Spirit of God dwells in you" (1 Corinthians 3:16).

It is important to continue to pursue God's presence with due diligence in prayer, until something happens. Within your being, the momentum of praise will usher you from the outer courts into the Holy of Holies. It is from this majestic throne that you will experience a streaming river of bliss that overflows and trickles from your upper consciousness into the reservoir of your soul. The riverbed of your being becomes inundated with the inner current of worship, which bursts into a stream of heavenly substance and springs forth as a mighty fountain. The Bible says, "Out of his belly shall flow rivers of living water" (John 7:38).

God's presence is accessible to all who thirst and desire to be filled. So, drink from the infinite well of the Supreme Being, who is able to quench your thirst and fill all things!

Affirmation

I now enter a deeper depth of devotion,
with my heart, mind, and soul.

CHAPTER 23

THREE ASPECTS
OF THE MIND

————————— ●■● —————————

Conscious Mind, Subconscious Mind, Superconscious Mind

There are three aspects of the mind: the conscious mind, the subconscious mind, and the superconscious mind. The conscious mind relies heavily on your five senses for understanding. It identifies with the appearance of the material world and its form. The conscious mind is also the director of your concentration, your attention, your focus, and the ideas that are impressed in your subconscious mind.

The conscious mind often interprets the world as reality but fails to look behind its appearance to discover its true nature. Again, the mind must be retrained to distinguish between reality and nonreality. This is accomplished by listening to the inner voice of your subconscious mind. Once your mind has been reoriented, you will not be influenced by external appearances.

Neither will you accept or entertain negative thoughts involving your life and personal affairs, such as, *You will never have a wholesome relationship*, or, *You will never be successful in anything you do*. These conditions of limitation and lack are what you create in your ignorance of the laws of creative thought, but they are not the ultimate will and plan of God for your life.

You must understand that negative thoughts, the idea of lack, and the limitations that you and others set for you are illusions that often influence your actions. You can stop placing restrictions on yourself by not accepting these negative thoughts as real or true.

While playing the game of life, you have the option of functioning from your superconscious mind so that you can recreate a life of abundance for yourself. This is God's divine plan for you, and there is an infinite supply for every demand. He will provide for your every perceived need because God is infinite abundance!

Never think, feel, speak, or accept negative impressions into your subconscious mind. Remember, you are the cocreator of your own experience. All acts of creation in this relative world are cocreating with God. In the absolute (spirit), we are creators—one with God.

Always think on positive things, in spite of the negatives that arise. Stay centered on God, who is within you. Never think about failure, lack, or limitations, and do not allow resentment, bitterness, hatred, jealousy, or criticism to occupy your mind. Above all, do not be judgmental of others because this will hinder your spiritual growth and development.

The way to stop negative thoughts is to purify your mind through self-reflection, meditation, and contemplation. So think, feel, and speak what you desire, and you will manifest it in the material world. Think health! Think wealth! Think abundance! Use these gifts for your success and for the benefit of others.

The subconscious mind is like a sponge. It absorbs and stores every experience that you have. The subconscious is in tune with your most intimate feelings and emotions. It is so powerful that it causes the human involuntary systems of the heart, digestion, and secretion to function without the attention of the conscious mind.

The intelligence of the subconscious mind reserves and retains vital actions of life. Deep within the recesses of your subconscious mind, patterns, habits, and instincts are carved, all of which can help you attune to a higher level of conscious awareness. The subconscious mind never forgets. It contains the unseen force behind the vibrations of thoughts and feelings, where all things are initially created before they manifest in the material world.

In general, the subconscious mind is influenced by the conscious mind. The subconscious will accept whatever is given to it by your conscious mind and bring that impression to pass if the thought and feeling are strong enough and retained long enough. This is one way that you can change or improve your life.

If you train your conscious mind and reeducate your subconscious mind, magnificent and amazing things will happen for you. You will live a richer and more fulfilling life. This is a direct result of educating and developing yourself in consciousness, which will eventually ground you in truth.

The untrained conscious mind often becomes a battlefield where positive thoughts are engaged in war with negative thoughts, which makes it a struggle to stay focused. There is an undercurrent of turmoil surging deep within your being. The increase of debris and the arsenal of bad thought arise. Such internal conflicts cause your judgment, rationale, and reasoning to be clouded and distorted, but with proper training, you can make positive changes to get positive results.

When thoughts and strong feelings are impressed on your subconscious mind, your subconscious will immediately begin processing them to manifest the predominant thought that is held in your conscious mind. The subconscious mind will respond faster to positive affirmations than to negative ones because it draws from the universal mind of God and produces exactly what you affirm or decree.

Elevating your consciousness to transform negative thoughts into positive ones is one of the keys to life's fulfillment. Again, the subconscious mind does not rationalize as the conscious mind does. However, the subconscious mind will labor ceaselessly to manifest your thoughts or feelings.

I cannot emphasize enough that the subconscious mind will accept any suggestion the conscious mind transfers to it, whether it is good or bad. Raising your level of awareness to the Christ consciousness will allow you to function in the full capacity of your mind and control or alter any emerging thoughts. When you operate from a higher consciousness, your awareness is keener, decisions are easily made, your ability to see reality is clearer, and your imagination becomes more creative.

God Himself imagined man. Out of that imagination, man became thought, thought was manifested into existence, and man appeared as a living soul. You are designed to be creative with your mind and think from a higher consciousness, which allows you to think beyond ordinary people. Thoughts of the mind are powerful when used in accordance with the creative spiritual laws of God—the unthinkable can happen!

I understand that it is a difficult task to retrain your mind to think differently than the way that you were previously conditioned. But now, it is time for you to recondition your mind and take control of your thoughts so that you will be in proper alignment with the creative forces of God. Such an alteration will prevent you from regressing to your old way of thinking.

A relapse can result in confusion, indecisiveness, doubtfulness, or double mindedness, which will adversely interrupt the creative process. Reconditioning your mind requires much patience, endurance, and sometimes suffering. This transformation can be achieved through hard work and by watching your own thoughts—thoughts that can alter your mental state and impinge on your higher good.

Think about the process of mental change as a metamorphic experience like a caterpillar evolves and develops into a butterfly. First, it wraps itself in a cocoon, where it is dark, lonely, and restricted. While in this state, transformation and maturation occur. Once the metamorphic process is complete, the butterfly breaks free from its restricted quarters of the cocoon and flies away gracefully with an array of beautiful colors.

People avoid this transformative process because they are challenged by having to detach themselves from people and things. These individuals believe that letting go of any kind is a painful experience, which is a false notion. These false notions automatically generate a feeling of separation and the deprivation of possessing things that once brought temporal pleasures. In general, people do not want to be without or forced out of their comfort zones and into unfamiliar territories.

This transformation requires change—changing old thoughts and habits. When you are stretched beyond your capacity of comfort, you will experience some degree of discomfort. The actual experience does not cause pain, but the thought of the experience causes the perceived pain.

People are uncomfortable with having to change who they think they are, when they really have no clue as to their identities. Oftentimes, people seek to validate their persons and existences through the false reality of identifying with tangible things. When their identities are not apparent, people may experience anxiety and frustration, which will eventually lead them down the path of depression or possibly self-destruction.

I can relate experiences (maybe you can too) where I encountered certain events that left me feeling emotionally drained, alone, trapped with nowhere to escape, confined to dark places of life with nobody to assist me in my wilderness experiences. Believe it or not, you create your own false sense of pain when you struggle against change. However, this perceived pain can be used to crack the shell that encloses your understanding.

Trials and tribulations of life expose you to the metamorphic process, which is designed to beautify and perfect you. It is your only solution. It does not seem that way at first, especially while you are going through it. Nonetheless, there is something amazing taking place within your soul—like a rebirth!

I understand that transforming is not an easy process. At times, it seems overwhelming and unbearable and appears that you are not going to survive it. Fret not because the dwelling God is always with you. He knows what is best for you and how much you can withstand. He will not allow you to be overwhelmed by the troubles of this world. In the appointed time and season, you will be delivered from the mental torment of your experiences.

Life experiences serve as teaching tools for the soul. As you glance in retrospect at all of your negative experiences and inner struggles, you then realize that God used them for your higher good. Oftentimes, discomfort serves as a catalyst for change. It ultimately makes you a new person with a new way of thinking and draws peace, happiness, and perfect health to you. The Bible says, "For as he thinketh in his heart, so is he" (Proverbs 23:7). A person literally becomes what he or she thinks. A person's character is the complete measure of all thoughts, and nothing will manifest without them.

The subconscious mind will reach forth into the universe and bring a resolution to every adverse condition and circumstance in your life so that life will become more fulfilling for you. It is like a magnet that attracts and draws the prominent thought that you are entertaining into your experience. So be careful what you think because the law of attraction is always in operation. Ensuring that you draw the thing that is consciously desired requires a moment-by-moment observation of thought and making the appropriate selection of the thought that is to be transmitted subconsciously.

Through this observation of conscious thinking, you will discover every truth connected with your being and come to the realization that you are the measure of your character, the maker of your life, and the director of your destiny. The degree of success depends on whole-brain-thinking, which involves both hemispheres of the brain.

Ordinarily, people think from either the left or right side of the brain at any given time. Only thinking from one side causes an imbalance in the thought process and takes you out of alignment with the balancing system of the universe. Even the stars, moon, and sun are governed by the force of symmetry, and you are a part of this symmetric energy. It will allow you to bring both hemispheres of the brain into balance and prevent you from having to function from one side only. Whole-brain-thinking can be achieved through various forms of meditation.

Half-brain thinking sends mixed signals into the universe and creates conflict and confusion between your subconscious and conscious mind. You become unstable like a pendulum on a clock, swinging from one hemisphere to the other and never coming to a place of equilibrium. Many people live in this way and wonder why they can never seem to stabilize their thoughts or make clear sound decisions regarding life's matters.

Aligning your thoughts with your spirit will help you avoid living a life of chaos. This alignment will help you enter into union with the Creator, where peace and serenity reside, and ultimately, it will offer you rest for your weary soul.

Calmness of mind is a characteristic of self-mastery. Both are attributes of wisdom. The presence of wisdom is a direct indication of true realization. It is far greater than ordinary knowledge. You become calm in your awareness; in that you understand yourself as a thinking being. Possessing such knowledge gives you understanding of others.

When the mind is fully developed, the understanding and ability for self-mastery will increase. You will cease frowning, feuding, worrying, or grieving. You will remain steadfast, unmovable, serene, and poised. It is said in scripture, "A man who rules his spirit is mightier than that man who takes a city" (Proverbs 16:32). The tranquil person, having learned to govern the thoughts, knows how to adjust appropriately. This will serve notice to that individual's spiritual strength.

The calmer you become, the more effective you can be in your sphere of influence. Those who are in your immediate presence will develop their self-control simply through association.

It is rare to find a person with such a noble quality and who has mastered that characteristic of self-control. Many people destroy such qualities by having an explosive temper, which literally destroys their posture of character, lives, relationships, and finally, happiness—all because they lack control. Only a small percentage of people live a well-balanced and structured life.

The nature of human beings burns with uncontrollable passions, unruly behaviors, fears, and doubts. But the human whose thoughts are governed by wisdom makes the wind and raging storms of his or her soul obedient. Whatever predicament you find yourself in, just anchor your soul in the still ocean of your inner being, and you will sail to the seashores of safety, where calmness exists.

Keep your focus firmly on the helm of thought because in the back of your mind, the commanding Master reclines, who is none other than your Christ consciousness. He is always in control. So speak to your heart and mind, *Peace be still*, and see the salvation of the Lord. Remember, self-control is strength, right thinking is mastery, and calmness is power.

Let us probe deeper into the dynamics of the mind and nature of thoughts. As previously mentioned, all thoughts, be they positive or negative, become suggestions, which are absorbed by the subconscious mind. For example, if you think you are healthy, wealthy, and wise, the subconscious mind will receive these thoughts and cause them to manifest in positive ways. In contrast, if you think that you are ill, worthless, poor, or anything else that is negative, the subconscious mind will receive these negative suggestions and cause them to appear in your experience.

You will continue to attract the same types of experiences, as long as you retain the sponsoring thoughts. So it is imperative to think positively and align your speech, emotions, and actions to match your positive thoughts. Thinking one thing and saying another or feeling one thing and acting in another way will prevent you from getting the results that you desire. This inner conflict confuses the subconscious mind, which only gives rise to chaos.

Refrain from listening to negative thoughts. It gives them the power to multiply. In order to avoid inner turmoil, it is necessary for you to control your conscious mind by always being aware of your thoughts and choosing only positive ones. When you do this, your feelings, speech, and actions will automatically reflect the suggested thought of the subconscious mind. Over a time, you will learn to master your thinking.

You can change any adverse situation in your life simply by not affirming it and embracing the positive aspects of the circumstance. Negativity is created when you do not know who you are. It brings disaster, disharmony, lack, and destruction. Elevate your mind and attune to your subconscious mind. A collaboration of the conscious and subconscious minds, accompanied by proper thinking, will make you more aware of your innate abilities to demonstrate the mind of Christ with poise, power, and peace. The goal is to develop and evolve spiritually so that you reflect the highest attribute of God, which is love.

Let us now look at the superconscious mind, which is an extraordinary aspect of your being. It is the God consciousness within you. The superconscious mind is all knowing. It has always existed within you, although you may not be aware of it. This divine mind summons you to journey on the inner path to a better, more fulfilling, and more qualitative life.

When you fail to listen to this inner voice or follow the direction of the superconscious mind, you create a detour that leads into the wilderness of life, causing sadness, misery, and disaster. So it is especially important to learn how and when to listen to the inner voice of your God consciousness. If you want to connect with the superconscious mind, you must train the conscious and subconscious to be still. This process of stillness is necessary for the transmittal of signals from the superconscious to the lesser mind.

You can retrieve a constant stream of supernatural information, as long as you remain connected to the superconscious mind. On a daily basis, it requires prayer, silence, and meditation. A method of ceaseless devotion will produce great momentum to your spiritual progress and lead you into the realm of the superconscious mind. The superconscious mind is the mind of God, which is the real you. It has divine intelligence, which works with our sympathetic and parasympathetic nervous system. It communicates with the conscious mind.

The superconscious mind has all the answers to any problems that may arise in your life. Your superconscious mind knows all about you—your past, present, and future. This great mind will always be a light on your inner path. It will guide and lead you as long as you listen to your inner voice.

Many have escaped tragedies by following their inner voices. I am sure that you have heard someone say, "Something told me not to go there," or, "I had a hunch that I shouldn't do it," only to discover later that all hell broke loose at the precise location he or she refrained from going to or doing something at.

Two voices constantly talk to you: your higher self and your lower self. You must decide which one you will follow because your decision determines your destiny from a relative perspective.

The negative voice from the lower self is always speaking and trying to trap you within its undertone of vibrations so that you will think along negative lines. Remember, negativity is drawn to you because it exists in your subconscious mind; otherwise, it cannot reach you. However, you are able to gain victory over such a condition, which sits deep within the crevice of your mind. I encourage you to first remove all negative thoughts and replace them with positive ones. Until this is accomplished, you will always be a victim to destructive and adverse conditions.

As you gradually take corrective measures to perfect your subconscious mind, you will become more aware of your superconscious mind and destroy all negative forces in your life. It is only when you eliminate negative thoughts that you will achieve self-mastery. As you perfect your subconscious mind, you disarm the destructive nature of the ego.

You can always detect positive or negative thoughts by how you feel emotionally. A positive thought is illuminating, and it always encourages, motivates, and edifies. Figuratively speaking, "God is light and in Him is no darkness" (1 John 1:5). Light always reflects the nature of God. Stay in this light, and you will always be protected. Evil will not come on you because darkness cannot appear where light exists. Bask in the presence of light. It will always keep you from falling back into the darkness of negative thoughts.

Watch, control, and alter your thoughts. Trace their effects upon you and others. Link the causes of your thoughts with their matching emotions. Contemplate every experience and outcome with patience and self-evaluation, as you go through life.

Affirmation

I now master the conscious mind and the subconscious mind. I take control of every thought within my superconscious mind.

CHAPTER 24

THE EGOCENTRIC MIND

— •■• —

Id, Ego, Superego

Every facet of life has its equivalent, just like the three levels of consciousness—the conscious, the subconscious, and the super conscious—have their counterparts: the id, ego, and superego. The id comprises the unorganized part of the personality that contains basic drives. The id acts according to the pleasure principle: It seeks to avoid pain or displeasure, and it is aroused only by increased stimulation of pleasurable sensations.

The id is conscious. It is the dark, inaccessible part of our personalities, and it constructs neurotic symptoms. Most of the symptoms are negative in character. The id can be described as a contrast to the ego, but it functions in conjunction with the ego. The id is chaotic and filled with energy, which comes from its instincts, but it has no organization. Id produces no collective will, but it strives to bring about satisfaction of instinctual needs.

The id is an antecedent to the ego. This innate apparatus begins at birth, a part of which then develops into the structured ego. The id contains everything that is inherited at birth. It is interwoven within the constitution of your physical makeup. Therefore, an instinct that originates from the somatic configuration is the first physical expression. For example, the mind of a newborn child is regarded as completely id ridden, in the sense that it is an accumulation of instinctive drives and impulses that require immediate satisfaction.

The id is responsible for basic drives. It knows no judgments, good, or evil, and it has no concept of morality. Instinctively, id is regarded as the great reservoir of the libido: the instinctive drive to generate life instincts, which are crucial to a pleasurable survival. Every individual possesses these instinctual impulses.

So let us see how the id interplays with the ego. The ego acts according to the reality principle: It seeks to please the id's drive-in, realistic ways. The ego attempts to mediate between the id and reality. It is often obliged to conceal the unconscious commands of the id with its own realization and to cloak the id's conflicts with reality.

The ego professes to notice reality, even when the id has remained rigid and unyielding. The ego comprises the organized part of the personality structure, which includes the differences of cognition, perception, and intellect. Conscious awareness resides in the ego, even though not all of the functioning aspects of the ego are conscious.

Originally, the definition of ego meant a sense of self, but this has been revised by various schools of thought in the academic arena of psychology. In modern English, ego has many meanings. It could mean one's self-esteem, an inflated sense of self-worth, or in philosophical terms, oneself.

The developed ego is known as the development of multiple processes: cognitive function, defenses, and interpersonal skills. Also, it could typically mean a set of psychic functions, such as judgment, tolerance, reality testing, control, planning, defense, intellectual functioning, and memory.

Essentially, the ego separates real things. It helps us arrange all our thoughts and makes sense of the world around us. Ego is the part of the id that has been modified by the external world direct influence. The ego represents what may be called reasoning or common sense, in contrast to the id, which contains the passion.

In its relationship to the id, the ego is like a man who is engaged in a wrestling match and who has to hold in check the superior strength of his opponent. In this instance, the id tries to compensate in its own strength, while the ego uses borrowed forces.

The ego serves three ruthless masters: the external world, the superego, and the id. Its task is to find balance between primitive drives and reality, while satisfying both the id and the superego.

The superego's main concern is with the individual's safety. It allows some of its desire to be expressed when consequences of a person's actions are insignificant.

Consequently, the ego is driven by the id, is confined by the superego, and is disgusted by reality. It struggles to bring harmony to the forces, external influences, and any other effects on it. When ego is under such demand, it voluntarily breaks out in relative anxiety regarding the outside world. In regard to the ego— It is moral anxiety, and in regard to the strength of the passion that is entrenched within the id is neurotic anxiety. The ego is constantly pressured by the danger that it might cause discontent on either side.

I allude to the fact that ego seems to be more loyal to the id. It prefers to overlook the finer details of reality and minimize conflicts while pretending to have a regard for reality. But the superego is constantly watching every move the ego makes. It waits to punish you with feelings of guilt, anxiety, and inferiority.

To rise above this, the ego employs defense mechanisms. The defense mechanisms are not employed directly or concisely. They are designed to minimize the tension by covering up impulses that are threatening. Ego defense mechanisms are often used by the ego when id behavior conflicts with reality, social morals, norms, taboos, or individual expectations, which come as a result of the internalization of these morals, norms, and their taboos.

Other defense mechanisms used by the ego are denial, displacement, fantasy, projection, reaction, regression, repression, compensation, and intellectualization. Sigmund Freud (1923) concluded,

The ego is not sharply separate from the id; its lower portion merges into it … But the repressed merges into the id as well and is merely a part of it. The repressed is only cut off sharply from the ego by the resistances of repression; it can communicate with the ego through the id.

This is where the superego comes into play. It acts as a parent to both the ego and id. Freud developed his concept of the superego by combining the ego idea and the special psychic agency, which performs the tasks of seeing egotistic fulfillment from the ego ideal and its insured (what is called your conscious). For him, the installation of the superego can be described as a successful instance of identification with the parental agency. The superego is influenced by those who have stepped into the position of parents, educators, and teachers and people elected as ideal models.

The superego aims at perfection. It encompasses the systematized part of the personality structure, largely but not entirely. It includes the individual ego ideals, spiritual goals, and the psychic agency (commonly called conscious), which criticizes and prohibits one's drives, fantasies, feelings, and actions.

The superego can be thought of as a type of conscience that punishes misbehavior with feelings of guilt. For example, taking somebody else's property when you know that it does not belong to you. The superego works in contradiction to the id. It strives to act in a sociable and appropriate manner, whereas the id just wants instant self-gratification. The superego controls your sense of right, wrong, and guilt. It helps you fit into society by getting you to act in socially acceptable ways. The superego's demands often oppose the id's demands, so the ego sometimes has a hard time reconciling the two.

The superego tends to stand in opposition to the desire of the id because of their conflicting objectives and its aggressiveness toward the ego. In general, the ego is a false sense of self. This sense of self believes that it is a human being and that it must fight for itself while engaging in daily activities.

The ego is operative within the human mind, and it is associated with the element of time. It compulsively thinks so that it will be assured of its future existence. The ego is slave to the intellect, operates from a place of conceit, and relies on things outside of itself. It serves as a kaleidoscope to the mind's mental eye, introducing false images that the mind thinks are true. It plays a persuasive part in the mental-perception process.

All people have a sense of self, which they identify with while developing in life. However, this sense of self is not real or constant. It changes often as external situations or circumstances change.

The ego is mostly detected in your possessive speech: my money, my car, my home, my job, my idea, my this, and my that. Most words are spoken from a place of me; however, nothing can really belong to anyone. The body that you live in does not belong to you, but it belongs to the Creator. You own nothing in this life. You only use what you have.

As for worldly possessions, I have never seen a hearse pulling a U-Haul trailer. You brought nothing into this world, and with certainty, you will take nothing out of it.

Ego not only stops you from discovering your true identity but also prevents you from becoming your spiritual self. Ego takes on many disguises and camouflages its presence within your personality to avoid detection. It has a way of tricking you and making you believe that it is a part of your makeup. Ego will initiate drastic measures to remain in control at all times. It is the true adversary.

Here is a phrase to think about: In me lies the enemy. The ego creates a false sense of separateness within your consciousness and spiritual self. The acronym for ego is "Ease God out." Ego is the place where negative thoughts are created, which have a direct influence on your behavior and attitude. It only produces selfishness, arrogance, boastfulness, vanity, and pride.

Ego is always seeking an audience to support and validate its existence by praise and acknowledgments. One of the greatest masters, Jesus the Christ, spoke much about the acts of the ego, which produce false pride to make others feel inferior while making itself feel superior. As a counteraction, He taught His disciples by demonstrating the attitude of humility through serving them and others. For example, He washed the disciples' feet, along with many other amazing miracles, healings, and feedings of the multitudes.

It is only in your Christ consciousness that you are able to demonstrate genuine servanthood and humility. Ego has no place in the face of humility, and it cannot exist there. The primary problem is that the false *I* (personality), which is constructed by the ego, is difficult to detect. But when you recognize the existence of the *I-ness*, it will be easier to surrender your false sense of self. You will rise above the natural realm of its inhabitance and into the spiritual realm of your higher existence.

The only way to dismantle the ego is by developing self-awareness on a conscious level. Attempting to dissolve this adversary is not easy, but it is a lifelong process.

It is believed that ego makes up the majority of the individual's personality (*I*). Ego permits you to express yourself in a diversified manner. There are many expressions that demonstrate individualism, but the primary, personality is considered the more authentic measure of your being.

It has been said that people are the product of their environments, including their immediate surroundings. Most individuals are taught and conditioned to believe, say, and do things a certain way. Unfortunately, it is easy to become addicted to and fixated on things that are learned. As a result, this behavior is perpetuated throughout society, causing a domino effect, which trickles down from generation to generation.

In general, personalities are formed by personal experiences and the influences that come from the world around you. Also, personalities are consolidated and solidified as a result of how you perceive and interpret your mental state while in the world. Relatively speaking, it is important to know that your experiences, whether good or bad, do not define who you are. In self-discovery and by way of your experiences, you are linked to realizations that define your identity.

Unbeknownst to you, you created the personalities that you are now experiencing, partly due to your cultural and social conditioning. These little *i's* of your personality are combined to form what many people call "me." Most may believe that without the I's there is no me. However, the reality is that only the true I abide in God's Spirit, the Super Consciousness, leaving all else false. All ego-based personalities vanish in the presence of the true I, leaving all other portions of your existence intact.

It can be difficult to do away with the things that you thought were you because you have lived with the idea your entire life. These personal I's are thought to be the thing that validates one's existence. Notice the use of the word *thought*, which is not who you are either. No one wants to lose something that is as important as being yourself, which is the first law of nature—self- preservation. However, if you are to experience life, you must first lose it.

Having to forsake all that you think you are and identify with the true I is one of the many challenges in life. This is real salvation: to put to rest all fabricated I's and to allow the real I to resurrect and emerge as the Great I Am. This is a blessed experience, even though Jesus did the initial work through His crucifixion, death, burial, and resurrection. You have a responsibility to work out your own soul's salvation. This is where the ego raises its ugly head to reserve a spot in your personality and destroy your efforts to transform.

The ego does not know the difference between transformation and annulations. It will fight the real you to maintain control. It does not want to surrender or submit to the God consciousness within. These false I's will try to ceaselessly impose, influence, convince, and persuade you that life is worthless without them. Unfortunately, human reasoning kicks in and causes you to revert to old mental patterns and behaviors, which make you more afraid to abandon all of your false I's (ego).

This cycle repeats itself, causing you to grip even stronger onto every ego-induced thought and never allowing the authentic self to emerge. The superego acts as the conscience and maintains your sense of morality and proscription from taboos. The superego retains the character of father, while the ego plays its role as mediator, and the id constantly reaches from the cradle like a baby who is seeking to fulfill its cravings and desires. This is the mental constitution of human beings.

Affirmation

I now bring perfect harmony to the three mental constitutions of my mind: the id, ego, and superego.

CHAPTER 25

PERFECTION

—————— •■• ——————

Perfection is an idea that most religions agree upon when determining what is right or wrong in the thoughts and conducts of their people. In spite of personal, social, cultural, and religious conditioning, people have consciences. They have something inside them that lets them know when they are going beyond the boundaries. This universal characteristic exists in all people, regardless of their religious beliefs. Humankind often puts a veil between its innermost conscience and its thoughts.

But if a person develops the capacity to see inwardly, even to some small degree, that individual will discover that a spiritual guide is present within. This guide tells that person what is right and wrong. This conscience emerges from a higher-quality state of mind, which is a direct reflection of a soul that exudes a force of life and energy. Since the primary desire of the soul's code is to return to God, this innate knowing of right and wrong is related to the human form, which is to be realized and lived out.

Jesus spoke of perfection in this way: "Be ye perfect even as your Father which is in heaven is perfect" (Matthew 5:48). God is perfection, and humans must reach human perfection. God's Spirit forms a divine union with your spirit, which formulates a total wholeness in the core of your existence. The Creator is perfectly pure in His love, which is unmixed with anything else. In His creation, He is the author and finisher of all, the intelligence within all, and the divine order overall.

Even though it seems as if imperfection exists on the outside, you remain perfect in your heart. If imperfection did not exist, there would be nothing to keep our souls here. All of our souls would immediately return to Him. Imperfection only exists because of perfection. Creation is exactly as He wants it to be. It is perfectly imperfect. Only those who have been enlightened by the Spirit dwelling in them will understand the divine qualities—the qualities Jesus Himself possessed.

Jesus was often called the perfect one. He was complete, faultless, and without defect. Moreover, since He is beyond all duality of creation, it can also be said that He is beyond perfection and imperfection. Saint John wrote, "In the beginning was the Word and the Word was with God and the Word was God" (John 1:1). From this perfection emanates the Word, the Son of God, and its manifestation in the Master.

The Master is perfection personified. He is perfect because of the word *Christ*—the perfect man, the perfect savior, the perfect Son, the perfect Christ, and the only begotten Son who is perfect in every way. The Word originally came through that voice, proceeded from on high, and reflected light below. The divine perfection of the Master is expressed in the physical world as human perfection. His disciples described their master's quality with evident affection and love. It is from a divine and perfect Savior that human beings receive the grace to become perfect too. Then as Jesus said, the disciple will become like his Master (see Luke 6:40).

No one person can become greater than the Master, but that individual can certainly reach the same spiritual level. This promise is echoed throughout Christian literature. For instance, Paul encourages a group in Corinth to strive for perfection. In an effort to achieve this realm of perfection, they will come face-to-face with human struggles. Everyone is automatically involved in these struggles, whether they like it or not. It is only perceived as a means to an end.

However, you must withdraw your attention from the world and your physical body inside yourself, with a single focus: to overcome innumerable human imperfections. All deficiencies distract the mind from its center and draw it downward and outward. Imperfections keep the mind and soul concerned with things of this world so that you cannot ascend to higher spiritual realms.

As you journey on your spiritual path, many obstacles will block your way. These obstacles are imperfect stairs that lead to the landing of perfection. Christ is the essence of perfection in an imperfect world so that we will be inspired. He will develop the qualities of His faultless nature at the human level. This is known as Divinity clothed in humanity, and it manifests harmony between the spirit and soul.

The spirit is always willing to express itself in the highest fashion while invoking the soul to extricate itself from the addictions of creation. Most addictions stem from the people's desire to gain something for themselves be it physical goods, personal motives, or sexual pleasures. The common goal is always the enhancement of the individual self, usually at the expense of others. In reality, this self does not exist.

When attention is attracted and is entrapped by unreality, it moves away from reality. In other words, when you become obsessed with anything other than the God within, you figuratively move from the Creator of your higher being and gravitate toward the appetite of your lower nature. The best and most effective approach in the quest for human perfection is to know that all that exists is perfect as it is, in spite of the human flaws.

In the presence of perfection, all imperfections are quickly identified. Like oil in water, they automatically rise to the surface. As Jesus said, "But seek ye first the Kingdom of God and His righteousness; and all these things shall be added unto you" (Matthew 6:33).

In preparation for uniting with God or entering a higher dimension, you must initially seek the internal God and His attributes, which comprise human perfection. He is the one whom all perfection comes from. But if you seek human perfection alone, you will only possess the inadequate means of personal struggle with the wish for material gain. Although you may have the potential and proclivity to acquire material things, you only need the essentials like food, clothing, and shelter for your physical existence. Many forget that possessing the basic necessities is only a means of sustaining life but that greed fosters obsession—wanting more and more and beyond the bounds of need.

This kind of obsession will lead to an intense attachment for the objects you have acquired. You suddenly become caught up in the illusion that all possessions are yours, not realizing that none of it can ever belong to you in any permanent way. They are only there for your use while living in this world. All belongs to God, from soul to substance. I admonish you to unite the lower aspect of your nature with the higher consciousness of your being so that it can lead and direct you into harmonious balance for perfection.

Affirmation

I am perfect and complete in every way. I
reflect the perfect God within me.

CHAPTER 26

SERENITY

—————————— ●■● ——————————

Serenity serves as a breather and a pause from life-challenging activities. However, when dealing with outside adversities, a great struggle emerges in your mind, which often distorts your judgment. As a result, you become your own casualty of war because you are a victim of chaotic thoughts.

Chaos is not always a negative thing. It can be used as a building material to construct peace and order in your life. Nothing in life goes to waste. There is a positive energy at the core of all things, which can be extracted from the worst of conditions.

Calmness of mind is a beautiful jewel of wisdom. It results from the patient effort in self-control. Its presence is an indication of ripened experience, which is more than ordinary knowledge and operations of thought. People become calm in the measure that they understand themselves, thought-evolved beings. Such knowledge necessitates understanding of the mechanical function of others and being able to see internal relations of activities by the action of cause and effect more clearly. This insight eliminates the chaos of fussing and feuding, while at the same time, it sanctions you to remain poised, steadfast, and serene. It is said that a man who controls his spirit is mightier than a man who rules a city.

Having learned to govern themselves, calm people know how to adapt to their environments and others. In turn, others revere their spiritual strength, seeking to learn from them, as well as rely on them. The more tranquil a man becomes, the greater is his success, influence, and power to exemplify good. Even the ordinary businessperson will discover prosperity in business affairs, as he or she develops a greater self-control and composure, for people always prefer to deal with someone whose behavior is strongly equable.

Strong, calm people are always loved and revered. They are like trees' shade or stable shelters in a storm. Who does not love a tranquil heart and a sweet-tempered, balanced life? It does not matter whether it rains, sleets, or shines. No matter what changes confront those possessing these qualities, they are always settled, serene, and calm. Excellent poise of character is the embryo of life, and it produces the soul.

Composure is precious as any earthly possession. It is a life that dwells beneath the waves in the ocean of truth and beyond the reach of tempest in eternal calm. Being still and silent will allow you to observe the undercurrent of turmoil that stirs you within.

How many people do you know who ruin their lives, destroy their characters, sabotage healthy relationships, and wreck all that is lovable and beautiful, by possessing a volatile temper? It is rare to find those who are well balanced in their demeanors and who have exquisite poise (which reflects characteristics of a Christ consciousness) and a polished character. This helps them avoid wrecking their lives and messing up their happiness due to a lack of self-control. Yes, humanity rushes forward with uncontrolled passion and unmanaged grief. It is thrust by anxiety and doubt. But only wise and tranquil people, whose thoughts are harnessed and neutralized, make the winds and the storms of the soul obey them.

In spite of your previous or current experience, the place that you may be at, the conditions that you may live under, be mindful of this: Keep your attention firmly on controlling your thoughts because in the back of your soul, the Commander in Chief reclines. He is the true Commanding Master. He is only in resting. Whisper to Him, and He will arise.

Affirmation

Self-control is strength, right thinking is mastery, and calmness is power. So say to your heart, "Peace be still."

CHAPTER 27

WHOLE AND COMPLETE

———————— •∎• ————————

Being whole and complete is an essential and common desire among people. But there are many Christians who live a fragmented life. They spend enormous amounts of time and effort trying to mend the broken pieces of their lives, without pinpointing the problem and not knowing where to start. So they go through life confused and frustrated. They hope to find a solution to their problems.

I, too, have been in a dark, lonely place, where life seems to be a cloud of gloom. This place leaves you feeling empty inside and gives you a sense of despair, even after having done everything in your power to correct the problem(s). It is quite easy to become discouraged and lose hope, as well as trying to make sense of everything that has taken place in your life. Yet you continue seeking God in prayer for a remedy and in hopes of being rescued from your dilemma(s).

The remedy is first realizing that you are complete in whatever stage of life you are presently experiencing. There are parts of you that you have not discovered. These parts lead you to believe that you are missing something. Everything you need already exists, but it has not been revealed or manifested to you. God created all things to be complete, especially humankind. So there is nothing fragmented about you, except in your thoughts. The notion of incompleteness stems from wrongful thinking, which leads to erroneous conclusions.

This type of thought is divisive, and it will cause your perception to become polarized, declining to the lower spectrum of your mind negative pole. In other words, you have created a mental split for yourself, which forces you to think and function from two extremes:

the positive and negative ranges of your mind. You become like a pendulum on a clock that swings constantly back and forth without stability. Many clinical and psychological professionals call this mental shift bipolar.

We all possess this trait to some degree, whether it is the private conversations that we have with ourselves, wavering between thoughts and ideas, or making decisions. The classification of this illness depends on the individual's ability to effectively manage and control his or her thoughts and actions. For example, if someone observed a person grasping at the sky for no apparent reason and talking aloud, that person would probably be considered mentally disturbed. But an individual who quietly whispers to him or herself shifts the direction that they are walking, would be considered normal and viewed as having a change of mind.

So the difference is that one person is capable of managing and monitoring his or her personality, whereas the other person is not. If you are considered normal and mentally stable, but you are experiencing a sense of incompleteness, a resolution is within your grasp. You can achieve wholeness by simply understanding your psychological makeup and unifying with your Christ consciousness. All forms of existence are complete and whole, even though humans are conditioned to see in part.

I will attempt to illustrate wholeness by using the numbers one through seven, which signify completion within the Judaic numeral system that are relative to the scale of life.

On = unity

Two = division

Three = perfection

Four = completion of perfection

Five = favor

Six = labor

Seven = completion, which indicates the transformation and transmutation that allow one to transition and elevate to a higher level of consciousness.

The number seven plays a significant role in scripture, as well as our natural state of being.

Seven trumpets (Revelation 8:2)

Seven heads (Revelation 17:3)

Seven crowns (Revelation 12:3)

Seven vials (Revelation 21:9)

Seven stars (Revelation 5:1)

Seven angels (Revelation 15:1–6)

Seven churches in Asia Minor (Revelation 1:4)

Seven last words from the cross of Christ's crucifixion (Luke 23:34)

Seven dispensations and ages

Seven days in one week

Seven colors in the rainbow

Seven cavities in a man's head

Seven octaves in a man's voice range

Seven centers in the organism of man (chakra)

Many other references to the number seven denote completion. At this level of rest, transformation and rebirth occur simultaneously, and they are called salvation. The seven scales of completion are likened to the musical scale on a piano, which is composed of seven keys that are labeled by seven notes in its natural order: C^1, D^2, E^3, F^4, G^5, A^6, and B^7. The scale is complete. In order to proceed to the next scale, one must strike the following key, known as a sharp or flat, which can be used as a transitional key (black key). The purpose of the transitional key is to allow for a time of rest while not interrupting the present melody.

So it is with the keys of life. You will discover your completeness in stages, as you ascend to a higher octave in consciousness. This is an opportunity to proceed with a means to measure your progress while in the process of evolving. Such rhythmical inclination generates an evolutionary process, which will drive you to a deeper depth in the dimension of your soul. Unfortunately, many wait until they are faced with a dilemma, as opposed to freely responding to the inner call.

If you voluntarily surrender to the evolving process, you become a new being in consciousness and mentally leave all broken, past thoughts and experiences behind. Figuratively speaking, you will pass from death to life and transfer from the ego of darkness to the kingdom of light.

Salvation is a melody of a mended soul. It is offered freely through the Christ consciousness, which is reflected by His symbolic death, burial, and resurrection. Undergoing this type of transformation can be incredibly challenging and difficult because it requires you to deny yourself and to abandon your thoughts, ideas, aspirations, concepts, and emotions¾all the components that make up who you think you are as a human being. Mentally entertaining this notion of losing your perceived identity may create an uncertainty about continuing the process. But if you are able to muster some courage and journey the scale of life (moving from one through seven), you will experience a complete makeover.

It is like clay in a potter's hands. He molds, shapes, and reforms us to become unique masterpieces. This procedure is necessary because it purges the impurities that are within you and removes fictitious things about you. This portion of the journey does not feel good; however, it is designed to make you a better person.

Now you have moved to the number eight, which means a new beginning. At this stage of your conversion, you are considered spiritually awakened to a small degree. Do not trick yourself into believing that you have fully awakened. You are just beginning to wipe the sleep from your eyes. So be careful and alert. Do not doze and go back into your sleep state.

By avoiding this pitfall of slumber, you are able to continue in upward mobility. This ultimately leads to the Christlike life—a life of truly being free. Remember, you must work out your own salvation with persistence and hard work.

Affirmation

I am now whole and complete in my God consciousness.

CHAPTER 28

WEALTH

—————— ●■● ——————

We are constantly reminded throughout scripture that God is our
infinite supply and that we can experience priceless treasures while
here on earth because all belongs to us by divine birthright. You have
the inherent ability to tap into this reservoir of unlimited supply
and manifest it in the material world by using thought from your
imagination, mental visualization, and the spoken word. The use of
the spoken word activates things within the universe.

There was a prophet named Isaiah who stated, "My word ... shall
not return unto me void, but it shall accomplish that which I please,
and it shall prosper in the thing whereto I sent it" (Isaiah 55:11). Words,
imagination, and thoughts are a tremendous combination, which
transmits an enormous vibratory force in shaping our bodies and affairs.

You may very well be facing a financial dilemma at this time.
You may have accrued overwhelming debt, bills are past due, and
you owe people. Fret not. Remember, the Creator is your supply,
and that supply is for every demand. In perfect faith, you must
act as if you were wealthy and would receive all that you need and
want through the power of thought and speech. In other words, see
yourself living from abundance.

Wealth can be accumulated in many different ways. The God
within has given you the power to create wealth, even though not
everyone will experience financial wealth. I am convinced that those
who execute these biblical principles will acquire all that they have to
offer. If you seek financial wealth, it is important to start first with
an inward search because the kingdom of God is within you. Do

this before attempting to manifest wealth so that you will become obsessed with the material world when you experience increase. The aspiration for increase is built within the nature of life. It is the basic impulse of creation.

All human behavior is predicated on the desire for increase. People are in search of more food and garments, better homes, lavish living, attractiveness, information, and enjoyment. Increase is a craving that most people experience. It is the urge of an indistinct intelligence within them to discover an expression outside of themselves. All of life's existence is governed under that inevitability for constant progression. Eventually, the increase of earthly possessions will cease and dissolve at the time of your physical departure—your death.

With this understanding, it would be wise to set your affections on eternal treasures, which will never fade but last for eternity. People intuitively know that they will not live in this physical body forever, but they are perpetually in pursuit of material gains.

That is okay because continuous increase is encouraged and declared by Jesus regarding the story of the talents. Jesus said, "For whosoever hath, to him shall be given, and he shall have more abundance; but whosoever hath not, from him shall be taken away even that he hath" (Mathew 13:11- 13). The want for increased riches is not a sin or a taboo, but it is merely the wish for a more abundant lifestyle. Most people are attracted to those who can offer them a better and more prosperous life. When you accentuate and place value on kingdom stuff, it will project itself as an impression of wealth in your reality and the earthly realm.

Wealth becomes contagious, it spreads to every area of your life and gives you the experience of kingdom living. You are destined for abundance because the Spirit of the inner God draws from the universal supply and produces accordingly to the demand of faith demonstrated by the practitioner. Through the single eye of faith, you must act as if you have already received your abundance. "And all things, whatsoever ye shall ask in prayer, believing, ye shall receive" (Matthew 21:22).

When using this method of prayer, keep in mind that your physical action must match your spoken word. If you ask for success and prepare for failure, you will get the result that you have prepared for and not the result that you originally requested. For example, if you ask for sickness to leave your body, but at the same time, you sulk and complain to others about how sick you are, you have just neutralized your words. You must see yourself as healthy, by virtue of the thing you have prepared for, asked for, and imagined, even when you cannot see the slightest sign of it.

Faith is the bridge that links the unseen to the seen. All things become possible when you bring speech and action into alignment. For the average person, trying to get into this spiritual vibration is no easy matter because of the adverse thoughts, doubts, and fears that often arise and rob you of your abundance. These negative intruders are considered the troops of the enemy-ego, and they must be put to flight.

It is time for you to repeat your affirmations concerning what you desire, while simultaneously expressing joy as if you have already received it.

Before they call, I will answer; and while they are yet speaking, I will hear. (Isaiah 65:24)

The thing that you desire already exists. The children of Israel were told that they could have all the land they could see. This is true of every man. You have only the land within your own mental vision. Every great work and big accomplishment have been brought into manifestation by mentally holding the desired image. Before the big achievement, you will experience perceptible failure and discouragement.

When they reached the Promised Land, the children of Israel were afraid to go into the land, for they said it was filled with giants who made them feel like grasshoppers. "And there we saw the giants ... and we were in our own sight as grasshoppers" (Numbers 13:33).

This is almost every person's experience. However, the one who knows spiritual laws and how to apply their principles is undisturbed by appearance, and one rejoices without tangible proof. Above all, that person holds fast to the vision, gives thanks in advance that the end is accomplished, and trusts that he or she has already received it. This type of clear vision pierces the world of matter and allows you to clearly see things as they really are—in the fourth-dimensional realm and completely perfect.

So you must hold the desired pattern in your mind of your journey's end and demand the manifestation that you have already mentally received, whether it is health or wealth. Sometimes you may need the assistance of others to agree and intercede for you while holding to the vision. You may be too close to your own affairs to recognize the true nature of appearances, which often hinders progress.

In most cases, it is much easier to *see* for someone when you are not in close proximity to the situation. Jesus said, "If two of you shall agree on earth as touching anything that they shall ask, it shall be done for them of my Father which is in heaven" (Matthew 18:19). Do not hesitate to ask for help if you feel yourself wavering. Because no man can fail if someone sees him successful.

Many great men attribute their success to their wives, brothers, relatives, or friends—somebody who believed in them without wavering from the current vision. For example, at times during my spiritual work, I became weary and worn out, due to cumbersome demands. It required much study, preparation, and prayer, along with having to function full time in a part-time capacity, with extraordinarily little help from others. I was wearing many hats to ensure that things ran smoothly and efficiently.

I continued to work in this manner for many years. I struggled under insurmountable pressures and became very discouraged and frustrated. I started complaining about my conditions to God and Joy, who morally supported me through those difficult times. The more I was persistent to achieve certain goals, the more difficult things became.

I tried everything, within my human capabilities, to rise above opposition and to fulfill my task as a spiritual leader, but my continuous efforts were of no avail. By this time, things had gotten worse. All financial resources had dried up. To prevent further deterioration of the spiritual mission, I had to expend more energy and draw from my own personal finances, which left me mentally drained and physically exhausted. I felt like my back was against the wall and that there was nowhere to escape.

I constantly cried out to God for His help. I was desperate! I went on a lengthy fast and prayed, seeking relief as well as a miracle. It seemed as though I was in a daze and functioning on autopilot. In addition, I worked an eight-hour job on a daily basis, which had its own stresses. As much as I wanted to end this escapade, I could not find it in me to do so. I kept pressing forward in hopes of finding a solution to my dilemma.

I sought counsel from many sources that I thought had the answer. I requested prayers from others, who did not know how to pray for themselves. I even tried implementing self-help programs that I believed would end all of my agony. Unfortunately, none of them worked. By this time, I felt as though my world had been turned upside down and all hope was lost.

Meanwhile, Joy encouraged me through the entire process. As she observed me struggling, she constantly spoke positive affirmations regarding the spiritual work and the blessing that God was about to release in my life for my faithful service to His people. I knew that what she was saying was true, but because of my emotional state, a part of me did not want to hear it. Thank God, she did not give in to my pity party or give up on me. She was determined to help me break free of these mental strongholds that prevented me from properly exercising my faith toward God for a breakthrough.

In the meantime, I became very depressed about the entire ordeal. Joy was right there like a ram in the bush. She endured my complaints, tantrums, hostile behavior, and anger, which were all directed at her. But she never wavered in her undying commitment to assist me during those challenging times. She interceded with prayer, believing God would change things for the better. Yet I was feeling very numb in my spirit-man. I had no desire to pray, read scripture, or even continue my spiritual endeavors. In spite of adversities, I kept my hand to the gospel plow.

This downward spiral went on for months, and then suddenly, a miracle happened. Prior to a midweek Bible study, I was told by the church administrator that there was someone waiting to see me. To my surprise, it was a former organist of the organization. After we greeted each other, he stated that he was the bearer of good news. He did not reveal any information right away, which left me in suspense. After stringing me along with casual conversation for about thirty minutes, he eventually disclosed the wonderful news. In one week, a check for $47,000 would be released to me. Immediately, my chin dropped in disbelief. I was taken by surprise, and I was speechless.

When I did speak, I kept saying, "Do you mean forty-seven hundred?"

He repeated, "Forty-seven *thousand.*"

It took a while for it to register. Finally, I accepted what was happening and that it was real. My prayer had been answered. I attribute it mostly to the fact that Joy had interceded for me through prayer. Also, her faith had stood in the absence of mine, to bring this miracle to fruition. Consequently, my faith, trust, and confidence were all restored. I am profoundly grateful for such a wonderful person. Even to this day, she is my greatest fan and supporter of all my spiritual endeavors.

Affirmation

I now tap into the wealth of my soul, where the
infinite supply of true abundance exists.

CHAPTER 29

FEAR

———————— ●■● ————————

Fear is a psychological state that exists in people's minds and plays a major role in influencing people's decision-making regarding life's activities. It appears in various forms, such as phobias, anxiety, being fidgety, and fretfulness. There are different types of fear, and it is not necessary to investigate every form. But fear comes into being when your perception of relationship is not clear, or it is threatened.

A relationship is not restricted to two individuals but between you and the natural world, between you and possessions, and between you and ideas. If that relationship is not fully understood, fear becomes a major issue because life configures relationships. To live is to be interrelated, and without relationship there is no life. Nothing can exist independently. So long as the mind is seeking separation, there must be some degree of fear, which is an illusion.

Fear only exists in relation to something or someone else: fear of death, fear of defeat, fear of loss, fear of failure, and fear of being mentally or physically hurt. The question is how does one eliminate fear? First of all, anything that is triumphed over has to be subjugated again and again. No problem can really be overcome or conquered; it can only be understood and brought into harmony with the rhythmic vibration of life. Conquering and overcoming are two completely different processes.

The overcoming process opposes, refutes, defends, and combats, which only creates further conflict. The conquering process leads to more confusion and deeper fear. The things that you resist will persist. If you attempt to understand the nature of fear and thoroughly examine and explore its content, it will never return in that particular form. However, fear will take on other forms in order to maintain its position and avoid detection, which is similar to the ego.

Again, fear is abstract. It exists only in the dynamics of relationships. Beyond that, it is easy to become afraid of not being and of not becoming. When there is fear of not being, not progressing, the unfamiliar, or death, can that fear be overcome by willpower and determination? Apparently, it cannot. Sheer suppression or substitution creates further resistance. That is why fear can never be defeated through any form of discipline, a defense mechanism, or resistance.

Therefore, no intellectual explanation will give you freedom from the dreadful grip of fear. Those facts must be observed, sensed, experienced, and finally, realized. What are you afraid of—a fact or an idea about the fact? Are you fearful of the thing as it is or what you believe it is? Take death, for instance. Are you frightened of death or the idea of death? Are you afraid of loneliness or the thought of loneliness, with its perceived aches and pains?

Inevitably, fear remains because you may have previously experienced it or some knowledge about it. Fear is obviously the result of words and terms that reflect what is being emotionally felt as fact. However, fact of fear is one thing, and the idea of fear is another. You must ask yourself, am I scared of the word *death* or death itself?

So you must determine exactly what you are afraid of. Is it the idea or the word? After identifying and mentally selecting the thing that is feared, you must face it with acceptance and understanding so that you can unmask the masquerade of fear and cause it to vanish. If you are afraid of a word, embrace it. Explore the term and its implications, as with any other form of fear.

The idea of fear is often reawakened due to previous knowledge, opinions, ideas, experiences, and trepidation regarding the fact— what the fact may be or do that creates fear.

You do not have to take ownership of the thing that you fear by labeling it. Nor do you need to judge, condemn, or hold an opinion about it.

Simply observe it with the intention of extracting meaning from it. This process is conducted through thought. Thought is a product of the past. It is expressed through signs, symbols, images, and verbalization, which are translated and interpreted by the mind. Thus, the mind creates fear and facilitates the process of thinking. Thinking is verbalization, whether it is constant chatter that takes place inside your head or speaking it aloud.

It is impossible to think without words, symbols, or images, all of which are translated and interpreted by the mind to produce prejudices and biases regarding previous knowledge that has been causally related to your current thought. During this translation process, the mind forms apprehensions about its interpretation and then projects it upon the fact. From that, fear arises.

However, there is freedom from this mental state of fear when the mind is able to comprehend the fact without translating it or giving it a name or label. This is relatively difficult to execute because your feelings, reactions, and anxieties are quickly identified by the mind and given a label. For example, the emotional feeling of anger is identified by that word or its synonyms.

So is it possible to experience and identify a feeling without naming it? It is the naming of the feeling that gives it power and permanence. The moment you put a title, label, or name on something that is rooted in and induced by fear, you strengthen it. However, if you are able to observe that feeling without giving it a term, you will see it fade away. Therefore, if you want to be completely free of fear and a false, delusional state of mind, it is important to understand the power and the use of labels, terms, images, symbols, and projections, as well as the nature of fear. Liberation dwells in self-knowledge. Self-knowledge is the beginning of wisdom, which is the ending of fear.

Affirmation

I now escape the shadows of fear and walk in the
light of love with peace and a sound mind.

CHAPTER 30

SEXUAL INTIMACY

●■●

Sexual intimacy always makes for good conversation. The question is often asked, "What's the difference between sex and making love?" Making love regularly consists of sex, whereas sex does not necessarily include making love. Sex is a physical activity that is directly intended to satisfy one's sexual desire. However, making love is more blissful when two individuals share in a positive give-and-take experience. It forms an emotional bond between the two individuals.

The sexual drive is the most powerful desire in the human expression, which is normally demonstrated in the act of making love. In fact, it can have a life-changing impact on you. It can possibly lead to conception with having the responsibility of raising a child. Furthermore, sexual intercourse produces binding ties between two individuals. These ties are much more intense than kisses, hugs, or sexual caressing. This inherent nature cannot really be explained, but you can instinctively sense it. Because of its powerful implication, it would be wise to try to control and regulate your love and sexual life.

Making love through the act of sex has a lot to do with your personal and spiritual development. In fact, ancient teachings talk about the art of lovemaking and sex as primary forms of personal and spiritual development, known as tantra. Personally, I have not attempted to engage in this particular system. However, in my own path of development, I mirror certain aspects of tantra.

You can use lovemaking as a foundation for personal and spiritual growth when it is performed in the proper context of spiritual matrimony—the two merging hearts. When both partners unify in this way, they become a mirror image of each other's lives.

The way you live is reflected in your sex life. If you are conservative in life and governed by societal norms, it is more than likely that you are considered dull, and your sex life is likely to be that way too. On the other hand, if you are adventurous and uninhibited in your lovemaking, then you probably live in a similar fashion. My point is that your life can teach you numerous things about your sex life and vice versa.

This principle of intimacy can produce the desired results, both in your life and in lovemaking through the act of sex. This same principle carries a certain type of energy that is expressed in the masculine and feminine gender, which is known as yin and yang. These terms are often used in the Far East to articulate the polarity that exists among the feminine aspect (yin) and the masculine aspect (yang).

The male and female principles are always in operation, flowing in sync with an emanating energy, which displays itself in various forms. The two energy aspects of lovemaking are interwoven in the fabric of life and all existing elements. Once you understand the dynamics of this phenomenal and energizing force, you will inevitably take your lovemaking to another level. It will usher you into the ecstasy of agape love. This experience will help you see life and you as complete and connected.

Though there are countless influences and powers in the world that reflect the Lord's reality and project illusions at the physical level, at this level, there is nothing more powerful than an individual's sex drive, which actually expresses that person's need for union with God.

Consequently, many are driven by this unharnessed passion to pursue sexual gratification with other individuals. People are not to live for sex because the body is primarily designed for seeking the indwelling God while here on Earth. Saint Paul said, "The body is not for sexual immorality but for the Lord, and the Lord for the body" (1 Corinthians 6:13).

Many crave such pleasure because it is associated with the warmth, affection, and companionship that normally exist between male and female. A relationship does not have to involve sex for intimacy to be present. Oftentimes, emotions are mistaken for love. Needless to say, love is independent of any emotion, although it can be expressed in the act of love.

Sexual intercourse is essential for procreation and is a strong, instinctive, biological urge. Without it, physical life would become extinct. Aside from a consecrated union of hearts, engaging in sex has its implication: It creates soul ties, which will interfere with the spiritual growth and development of individuals. The more powerful the desire, the deeper the binding is physically.

No one can deny the intense nature of sex because it is the gift of human pleasure and reproduction from God. It can be spiritually beneficial when it is performed within the confines of a sacred divine union—between the male and female hearts.

Sex is universal, even among the animal and plant kingdoms. It is important to understand the misuse of the gift of sex. It can cause a person to regress spiritually and keeps the individual bound to the influential forces of his or her lower nature. To avoid this kind of influence, one must redirect one's energies to prevent a counterproductive episode and not entertain or provoke such a powerful force. It can become disastrous and ruin a harmonious relationship. My mother once said to me "One night of pleasure can cause a lifetime of pain."

Nonetheless, the very act of sex requires an enormous amount of energy, which pulls mental attention downward and makes it difficult for the spiritual practitioner to focus or experience the bliss of meditation. But with loss of this life-force energy, the act of meditation becomes fruitless.

The seed of a man is known to assist him for further enlightenment when channeled correctly. This seed is powerful in nature, in that it can create another human being. The initial enlightenment process begins when the man's testicles are filled with spermatic fluid, which is retained for a period, recycled, and then transferred upward through the spine and into the penal gland of the brain. This causes a chemical reaction, which normally induces mental insight, spiritual revelation, and illumination.

If this life-force energy fails to ascend, the eye of the soul will remain shut, causing spiritual blindness and leaving the individual as a prisoner to his own desires. Most men lack the discipline to refrain from releasing this fluid, due to their uncontrollable craving for sex. Some release by way of dreams and others by masturbation. Nonetheless, any method used to release this fluid takes away from energies that are normally used by the body for maintaining good health.

Loss of this energy has various negative effects, such as an inability to focus and concentrate, reduced mental alertness, diminished physical stamina, and a host of other adverse conditions. Athletes are instructed to refrain from sexual activity because of the adverse effects it will have on the body.

For many, it is a difficult challenge to abstain from sex so abruptly, along with having other attachments. Abstinence is a gradual process to master because of a man's natural impulses. As people attempt to refrain from sex by the force of their wills while still struggling with inward desires, they will eventually fail in their efforts, and the urge of sexual desire will be even greater. This part of nature can be controlled, and it can have lasting results, when the individual connects to his or her higher self and rises beyond his or her lower self (flesh).

When you are caught up in the heavenly realm of consciousness, you enter the dimension of bliss and wonder. All desire for physical gratification diminishes and fades away like the day into the night. Although sexual intercourse is seemingly all physical, theoretically speaking, sex is 90 percent spiritual and 10 percent physical. From another perspective, your desire for sex is nothing but an act of penetration.

A figurative penetration has to take place in your own inner being, which means that you must go into yourself spiritually through meditation. There you will experience an endless spiritual climax. There is no physical thrill that can match it or measure up to it. When spiritual intercourse is in progress between the aspects of your being, you become whole, unified, and ultimately, one with God. All desire for the outer pleasures vanishes, freeing you from sexual bondage.

But when a man and woman physically and sexually connect, the act becomes superficial, even though it produces moments of pleasure for a short time. If you want to experience a long-lasting relationship that is fulfilling and satisfying, seek intimacy with the inner God of your soul.

Affirmation

I am the temple of God, where the soul and spirit
of my being unite in divine intimacy.

CHAPTER 31

AGAPE LOVE

●■●

Love is absolute in nature and unlimited, but it is expressed in relative and limited ways. In fact, it is the most powerful existence in the human experience. When you prevent love from flowing in its supernatural state and a relative mode, you create conditional love that is dependent on something or someone else. Countless types of love are conditionally based and are displayed throughout humanity in this manner.

Authentic love is rare, and it is difficult to find the words to describe this state of being. However, there are numerous attributes that reflect unconditional and limitlessness love: joy, inner peace, gratitude, acceptance, awareness, consciousness, presence, freedom, balance, and ecstasy. All of these are expressed in unconditional ways but in relative forms.

Genuine love is the key to be complete and whole within your core being and without needing outside validation. Once you have reached this level of consciousness, you will be able to function from your most basic nature, detaching yourself from the bondage of relative forms and its conditions. In other words, you will realize that you are love, and love is God, and God is love, and that is all there is, which is your true identity.

You are the I am, absolute reality and truth, and the source and life. Making a suitable love definition is quite a challenge. Love is so comprehensive that it barely lends itself to a definition.

In my search to know what love was, I first had to find out what love was not, which made up the whole in the context of love.

Speaking from a relative point of view, you cannot have *what is* without *what's not*. And from an absolute perspective, the two are the same. They are one in existence, being neither conditional nor unconditional. Love in its entirety encompasses both spectrums.

The essence of true love is unknown. In order to know it, you must eliminate its mystery. The unknown cannot be discovered by a mind full of notions. Initially, you must empty your head of thoughts that create them. Once you have freed your mind of its false notion with a nonjudgmental view, you know the true substance of love.

Let us first look at some of the conditional notions that create limits to the expression of love or the what's not. These conditional versions of love can be best described as relative in nature. They foster behaviors that demonstrate lower emotional vibrations, such as being judgmental, selfish, nonaccepting, cynical, frustrated, resentful, hateful, fearful, shameful, jealous, and depressed. The different versions of love cover the totality of human emotions. You can safely say that love is, in fact, the only source from which feelings and emotions surface.

People often equate emotions and feelings as love; therefore, they feel at ease to voice the phrase, "I love you." What do they really mean? Do they mean they have a certain attachment or feeling about a person? Or do they mean that they are codependent, as it involves somebody else? If so, they might want to reevaluate their views of love.

Most people use the phrase 'I love you loosely', which is solely based on their selfish desires and underline motives. In other words, most people associate love with what another person can do for them, by catering to their expectations. This distorted perception of love can create a problem for the recipient and the reciprocator. Here is why. The reciprocator unconsciously gives with the expectation of receiving something in return, while the recipient feels obligated to respond to the reciprocator's wishes. This is where the problem begins. Because of their erroneous outlook on love coupled with the act of giving and receiving, the reciprocator and recipient will instinctively claim each other as being each other's possession.

From possession, jealousy arises because the perceived possession is no longer attached to the notion of ownership, which causes certain emotions to be displayed. For example, suppose the person you have affections for is no longer willing to be in a relationship with you. Selfishly, you refuse to let go and accept what is happening. You relentlessly hold on to an image of that person in your mind. Meanwhile, you begin to develop feelings of anger, bitterness, or resentment toward that person, which demonstrates the very attitude of possessing. Mental holding of any sort implies that you possess that person through thought.

Jealousy and fear are not the only negative offspring of possession. There are a host of others that promote internal behavioral conflict. Consequently, we can accurately conclude that selfish possession is not love. Love is not how and what you feel, nor is it sentimental or emotional. The two are merely sensations.

Sensations are associated with the senses of an organ. Senses stimulate and stir certain emotions, which is not love. Emotions are an expression of feelings, and feelings reflect thought, and thought is a direct result of sensation, which causes inner conflict. A person who functions from a sentimental and emotional state cannot truly know love.

Are we not emotional and sentimental beings? Yes, but an emotional and sentimental person can be malicious in attitude when his or her sentiments are not responded to or when it appears that there is no outlet to express his or her feelings. As for the emotional person, he or she can be driven to hatred, strife, war, and self-destruction, simply from sentimental feelings. That is not love.

A person may seek a remedy for these behaviors and think forgiveness is the cure for all. Forgiveness implies that you insulted me, and I resent it and store it in my memory. Afterward, you seek my forgiveness, and I say, "I forgive you," which means that I am important and the center figure here. I forgive someone else. As long as this type of forgiveness is in operation, it accentuates the I as important rather than the person who insulted me. It is not love.

An individual who properly loves possesses no inner conflict, and he is indifferent to all negative emotions such as fear, jealousy, sorrow, forgiveness, and the importance of I. These emotions are the entire carnal mind. The carnal mind is enmity to God (higher consciousness) because it interprets and analyzes parts of the possessiveness, both of which are simply possessiveness disguised in various forms. These forms of possessiveness cannot give birth to true love but can only corrupt it. You can talk, sing, write, or even dream about it, but it is not love.

Respect is another distorted point of view to this idea of love, even though respect is shown in genuine love. You might have a respect for what a person represents but not respect for the person, and that is not love. When a person fails to be kind to a person and favors another based on his or her possessions or status, is considered to be partiality and not love.

In most cases, people are quick to cater to those with power, prestige, fame, and riches. Especially to anyone who can provide them with the means to live a well-to-do life. You say that you have respect for all, but it is only for those who are superior to you, and that is because you are out to get something. Genuine respect would cause you to revere those of lower social status as well as the so-called upper class. Where there is partiality, favoritism, and discrimination, there is no love.

Unfortunately, most of us fall into this category. We are selfishly possessive and full of sentiment and emotions that are subject to change, especially when accompanied by negative intentions. You will come to know love when all these negative behaviors cease, such as possessing, restricting, claiming, or expecting something against another's will. If you are in the possessive state of consciousness, it is impossible for you to receive positive results, being that it stems from the me construct—a place of selfishness.

How many of us are truly generous, forgiving, compassionate, and merciful? Do you demonstrate these attributes only when you are getting something in return as a form of payment? When these things fade away from your mind and no longer occupy and fill your heart, authentic love will spring forth.

Love alone can liberate you from the plague of selfish insanities in the world today, including religions, organizations, summons, programs, or theories. Love can only exist when you do not possess and are not jealous, envious, or greedy, but rather when you are compassionate and considerate of others, with the intent to serve the lowest to the highest and without looking for something in return. Love cannot be pondered, rehearsed, or systematized because those acts are still byproducts of the mind.

Again, when all of these states have ceased, love comes into being and emanates from your nature. Love respects one or many and knows no partiality because in the essence of love, there is neither one nor many but only love.

Let us peer deeper into the nature of love. Love is a word that is often used freely and greatly misunderstood. It seems to have lost its true meaning. Many been inspired in love through the written scripture, which says, "A new commandment I give unto you, that you love one another; as I have loved you, that you also love one another" (John 13:34). Love is the essence of God and the divine phenomenon that extends from the super conscious to the third dimension of the universe. Paul had a similar experience. "I know a man in Christ who fourteen years ago—whether in the body I do not know, whether out of the body I do not know, God knows—such a one was caught up to the third heaven" (2 Corinthians 12:2–4).

Real love is selfless and free from fear. It pours itself out upon the object of its affection without demanding anything in return and continually unfurls in the act of giving. Love is divinity in action through humanity and the strongest magnetic force in the universe. Pure, unselfish love attracts its own to itself. It does not need to seek or demand.

Real love is rarely demonstrated because of man's inability to conceptualize such a phenomenon. People are selfish, tyrannical, and fearful in their affections, thereby losing the thing that they love. To love when you are loved is humanity, but to love when you are not loved is divinity.

I remember when a close friend of mine came to me in great distress. The woman that he loved so much had threatened to divorce him for untold reasons. He was torn by hurt, anger, and resentment. I explained to him, "In order to receive perfect love, you must give perfect love. Perfect yourself on this woman; give her perfect, unselfish love, demanding nothing in return. Do not criticize or condemn her. Instead, bless her, wherever she is physically or mentally."

This was exceedingly difficult for him to do at first, but with time, he finally accepted the idea of a divorce and saluted her with his blessings. He then realized that loving someone might mean letting that person go mentally as well as physically. After all that was said and done, he was able to experience happiness and fulfillment as he had in the beginning of the relationship.

Invariably, your deepest fears will appear if they are not counterbalanced. The biblical character Job said, "For the thing which I greatly feared is come upon me, and that which I was afraid of is come unto me" (Job 3:25). Many religious people speak more of the fear of God than His love. They worship Him out of fear of being punished, either in this world or in hell. They hope for a reward in some heavenly place after death. They are afraid that if they do not worship Him, some calamity or misfortune will befall them in this life. This kind of fear has commonly been encouraged and preached from the pulpit of many churches. Some people even talk of "putting the fear of God" into someone. This is a negative kind of love, and it possesses little value.

The love of God gives a person understanding of all things and a sense of confidence that there is nothing left to fear, not even death or loss of things or people. The only fear that is needed is not fear at all. It is a godly fear, or reverence, that prompts one to honor and worship Him without trepidation. Just as you do not like to offend or hurt those in this world whom you love, you certainly do not want to offend your Creator. Love is ultimately the only true reality in the soul's relationship with God.

When you cast forth real love, it will return to you because the law of sowing and reaping (attraction) is always in operation. Unfortunately, most people have to experience some degree of opposition before they even get a glimpse of real love. Suffering is not necessary for man's development, but it is the result of violating spiritual laws. Without it, few people seem to be able to rouse themselves from their soul sleep.

Individuals often suffer loss because of a lack of appreciation. Follow the path of love, and all things are added. God is love, an invaluable substance that many waters cannot quench. Authentic love can never be priced. Although it seems to be a lost attribute, humans, with the knowledge of spiritual law, know it must be regained, for without it, they become as sounding brass and tinkling cymbals.

Scripture and other spiritual references clearly tell us how to dispense unconditional love. Christ served as a perfect pattern. He sacrificed Himself for all humanity: alcoholics, drug addicts, pimps, prostitutes, dope pushers, thieves, and murderers.

The essential nature of God is love, and from this love all His qualities spring forth. Now if God is love and the soul is created out of God's essence, the innermost nature of the soul must also be that of love. Our true relationship to God is love, and the pathway to the dwelling God is through Christ—the path of love.

The highest relationship of your soul is that of love. This wonderful gift is the best approach to everything and everyone in this world, no matter the situation or circumstance. Since God is love, and circumference is all, nothing else exists besides Him. All else serves as a reflection.

Saint John penned some profound words: "Behold, what manner of love the Father hath bestowed upon us, that we should be called the sons of God" (1 John 3:1). Just as a child is born of a woman, a soul originates in God. All souls are children of God. This relationship is based on true love for the Father. Jesus explained to His disciples that they were the children of God.

Again, John opens it up by writing,

Ye are of God, little children. We are of God ... Beloved, let us love one another: For love is of God; and everyone that love is born of God and know God. He that love not; know not God for God is love. Beloved, if God so loved us, we ought to love one another. If we love one another, God dwell in us and His love is perfected in us. God is love; and he that dwell in love dwell in God and God in him. We love Him because He first loved us; If a man says, "I love God," and hate his brother, he is a liar; for he that love not his brother whom he hath seen, how can he love God whom he hath not seen? And these commandments have we from him, "That he who loves God, loves his brother also." (1 John 4:6–8, 11–12, 16, 19–20).

We are commanded to love God with all our hearts, minds, and souls and our neighbors as ourselves (Matthew 22:37–40). The inclination of the soul is always toward the Lord, for love is constantly attracted by love. But without it, thoughts, desires, and feelings are more directed toward the world's activities. The heart becomes filled with human selfishness, worldliness, pride, anger, greed, lust, jealousy, and all kinds of attachments that leave little or no space for experiencing the real love of God. As a consequence, your attention and love are drawn into the world and away from God, and you find yourself becoming a lover of the world rather than a lover of God.

Seeking love in the wrong places can be detrimental to your well-being. To acquire such a love, you must first cleanse the mind of all negative thoughts and turn it toward the God consciousness. Only then does it become possible to follow the second commandment: loving your neighbor as yourself. It is not possible to simultaneously love your personal sense of ego and that of other people's, for the two are mutually at variance with each other. When you realize the

God within, you will discover that the real self is God residing in your spirit and not the individual ego or personality.

You are the essence of God, which allows you to see Him everywhere and in everyone. His love is omnipresent. So being filled with His love, you will love everything and everybody, treating all with respect, kindness, and understanding. There is no greater human quality than being able to love your neighbor as yourself. A neighbor is not only one who lives next door but also everybody with whom you come in contact. There can never be any restrictions, parameters, or boundaries on this kind of love because it is a universal expression. This gift costs nothing but has the greatest value. It can be shared among all people in all cultures. Act now! Share this powerful gift of love.

Affirmation

I am now a vessel filled with the light of God, which demonstrates authentic love toward all humanity.

CHAPTER 32

THE CHRIST CONSCIOUSNESS

— •■• —

The Christ consciousness is an exalted state that Jesus cultivated within Himself. If we were to implement such an ideal and channel the use of our creative energies, we would be given more than enough help from that ideal to change our lives. When we work with an idea and that ideal works with us, it is called the action of correspondence. However, the incarnation of God exists in all of us. That was what was so special about Jesus: He was directly aware of His oneness with the Creator.

This awareness was not only a theory or a concept but also a living reality. Jesus fulfilled God's intention while in human form. Simultaneously, He lived in oneness with God in a three-dimensional consciousness. Jesus mastered all levels of experience: His earthly death and heavenly rebirth.

In His teachings, Jesus made numerous implications regarding the topics of death and rebirth. This idea of death and rebirth is like an internal seed. It must concede itself to the enclosed shell and crack open before the plant is to spring forth. The kingdom of heaven lies within, waiting patiently for us to die spiritually to its presence.

We put this process into practice every night as we physically fall asleep and journey into the soul's consciousness—a mental state that consists of infinite love, peace, and tranquility. While in this changed state of consciousness, we experience oneness with the essence of life without being consciously aware of it. However, the result of such experience will certainly cause us to adjust our core values. We become less concerned with material things, power, prestige, and wealth. We feel at peace with ourselves, and we are more interested in the quality of our daily occurrences.

We will discover that we are more naturally concerned with the well-being of others, and we spend quality time to interact with them. In fact, we are able to witness our presence having a positive influence and impact on others in ways that we never imagined. When we focus on the needs of others, we don't focus on our own personal matters.

The development of Christ consciousness does not necessarily involve a striking spark of light. Also, the surrendering of the basic self does not always mean a total renunciation of our personal concerns. It can imply moving out of our own way; getting past self-induced addictions, attachments, and fixations; and making allowances for serving others.

The Christ consciousness is concealed within the minds of us all. In spite of our particular religion or faith, we do not have to suffer crucifixion at the cross in order to develop the Christ consciousness. We can learn from experiences that open our minds up to a fuller understanding of our ideal. Our mindset is the key to the Christ consciousness.

We live in a three-dimensional world where we experience God as Father, Son, and Holy Spirit, depending on your religious affiliations. Likewise, as humans, we are comprised of body, mind, and soul. We can equate this to:

The Father aspect of God is our bodies.

The Holy Spirit is our souls.

The Son is our minds.

In other words, the mind is like the Son of God. Such equivalence makes the mind appear exceptionally important and reveals this spiritual significance.

Jesus declared that nobody could get to God except through Him, even though every human being was part of God. Even so, we can experience God directly through the conciliator of our higher selves, as we grow in the Christ consciousness. This growth demands that every atom in the body resonates harmoniously with the ideal. The conscious mind plays a vital role in this development. The conscious mind decides to work with an idea. It focuses our attention on constructively developing the attitude as well as the habits. It also invites into awareness the deeper level of consciousness.

The conscious mind can direct the progression of the will so that it is in accord with the ideal. In scripture, Paul announces that although he desires to do right, he often does otherwise. He concludes that he must die daily in order for Christ to live within him. In other words, he opts to yield to his higher consciousness to develop his will. He imagines and believes that this higher consciousness will emerge to direct his every action.

While at the crossroads of choice, it is necessary to make a conscious decision as to what ideal we will serve. In turn, the ideal will assist us in our efforts to establish the Christ consciousness as the archetypal pattern in the universal mind—that Jesus died for our sins. This infers that He established a way for the physical body and consciousness to submit to God's will. The way He established this is now available as a pattern in a higher dimensional domain of ideas and ideals. It is within the superconscious mind. It is capable of influencing and guiding our own consciousness if we choose to invite it to.

We are like flowers. We draw on the radiant energy of the sun and pattern it in our own way to create love offerings of exquisiteness to those we interact with. The inconceivable powers of the mind are there for us to utilize as we choose to, although each of us perceives the world with a distinctively creative subjectivity.

How we view things and react to them determines the outcome of our experience. With our imagination, we can mentally contact the infinite realm of possibilities and transmit an affirmation on whatever goes with our vision. If we are willing to make a concerted effort, we can channel the creative, impending energy of that vision into a living reality. When we focus our attention on the highest principles' intention and extend ourselves to share our best efforts with others, we create a path that allows life energy to journey into new patterns of being. Our own awareness is expanded as we become channels of our higher selves and servants of our souls' mission toward our long-lost paradise while on earth.

If you feel this could be your ideal, if you can imagine it, if you are willing, act as if it were so, knowing that the thoughts of your mind will come to pass. That is the way of the Christ-conscious mind.

Affirmation

I am now infused with deliberate intention and willingness, by the Spirit of God, to awaken the Christ consciousness within me.

REFERENCE

———————●■●———————

Freud, S. (1923). The Ego and the Id. In J. Strachey et al. (Trans.), The Standard Edition of the Complete Psychological Works of Sigmund Freud, Volume XIX. London: Hogarth Press.

Printed in the United States
by Baker & Taylor Publisher Services